fired up with raku

over 300 raku recipes

irene poulton

the crowood press

First published in 2006 by
The Crowood Press Ltd
Ramsbury, Marlborough
Wiltshire SN8 2HR

www.crowood.com

British Library Cataloguing-in-Publication Data
A catalogue record for this book is available from the British Library.

ISBN 1 86126 848 3
EAN 978 1 86126 848 8

Disclaimer
Raku firing can be hazardous and it is important that correct health and safety pro-
cedures are adhered to and manufacturers' guidelines followed. The author and the
publisher do not accept responsibility or liability in any manner whatsoever for any
error or omission, nor any loss, damage, injury or adverse outcome of any kind
incurred as a result of the use of the information contained in this book or any
reliance upon it. Due to print media constraints some glaze colours shown will vary.

Acknowledgements
The following people and organizations have helped over the years to accumulate glazes
and other information: Wally Asselberghs, Belgium (www.wallyasselberghs.be);
Barry Crocker, Australia; Clayart (www.ceramics.org/cic/clayart); Dewitts Glazes
(www.dinoclay.com/info/glazes/degraku); Dinoclay (www.dinoclay.com); Mike Kusnik,
OAM (Australia); Carol Ratliff (www.ratliffpotteryandtile.com). In Chapter 4 I particularly thank Walker Ceramics (Australia) Pty Ltd for kindly allowing me to include
the tabular information on frits (for further information go to their web site at
www.walkerceramics.com.au or contact them direct at: 55 Lusher Road, Croydon,
Victoria, Australia 3136; telephone: +61 (3) 9725 7255; fax: +61 (3) 9725 2289).

Except where otherwise stated, photographs are by the author (in Chapter 7,
by the relevant artist in each case).

Photograph previous page: 'Shards of Memory'. (Photo: Victor France)

Typeset and designed by D & N Publishing
Lambourn Woodlands, Hungerford, Berkshire.

Printed and bound in Singapore by Craft Print International.

CONTENTS

1 What Is Raku? 7

2 Raku Firing and Raku Kilns 13

3 Raku Techniques and Problems 19

   Health and Safety for Raku 25

4 Raku Glazes A–Z 27

5 Alternative Methods and Materials of Decoration 79

6 Invited Artists 99

Appendix: Substitute Materials and Alternative
Names, Colouring Oxides and Conversions 137

Bibliography 140

Glossary 141

Index 143

1 WHAT IS RAKU?

ORIGINS

The origin of raku can be traced back to sixteenth-century Japan and the tea ceremony. The name *rakuyaki* or *raku* denotes a type of Japanese pottery, which involves low firing temperatures and the removal of pieces from the kiln while still glowing hot. In the traditional Japanese firing process, the pot or bowl is removed from the hot kiln and put direct into water or allowed to cool in the open air. Raku is recognized as the traditional method for creating clay bowls for the tea ceremony. These raku bowls are hand-made from earthenware and, due to the low firing temperature, have a porous body and were usually decorated by using a lead-based glaze. Some of these tea bowls are highly prized, each having a distinct form and individual style.

It was during the late sixteenth century that these raku artist potters were able to rise above the general craft potter of Japan with the formal recognition of their skills. The name *raku* is derived from the kanji character which means 'enjoyment' or 'ease'. It was during this century that Chojir, first of a long line of raku potters, came under the patronage of the tea master Sen-No-Rikyu. In 1598 the ruler Hideyoshi bestowed the name Raku on Chojir after he began making tea bowls to the great tea master's specifications. Upon the death of Chojir in 1592, his son Jokei continued the raku tradition. Both the name and the ceramic style have been passed down by the Raku family and continue to the present.

OPPOSITE: 'Maenad'. PHOTO: VICTOR FRANCE

Raku as it is practised today in the West bears only a little resemblance to the original method used for tea ceremony bowls. Paul Soldner, the American potter, is credited with westernizing this traditional practice sometime in the middle of the last century. The use of a reduction chamber at the end of the raku firing was introduced by him to compensate for the difference in atmosphere between the original, wood-fired, Japanese raku kilns and the more up-to-date gas-fired American kilns. Typically, pieces removed from the hot kiln are placed in chambers full of a combustible material, such as straw, sawdust or newspaper, which then provides a reducing atmosphere for the glaze, and to expose the unglazed clay surface to the black carbon. The use of lead in a glaze is now discouraged since it is toxic, but almost any low-fired glaze can be used.

CONTEMPORARY METHODS

But the methods used in raku today are still similar, in that the piece is first bisque-fired and then glazed and placed in a raku kiln and fired to approximately 1000°C, at which time the piece is taken from the kiln, while still glowing red, and placed in an airtight container. Sawdust, leaves or shredded paper and various other inflammable materials may be used to cover the piece after which a lid is placed over the top of the container, which is then left, depending on the size of the work, for anything from 10min to an hour to cool. This process is not without risk to the piece, the thermal shock of such a rapid transition from 1000°C can and often does shatter the piece.

The effects on the glaze are unpredictable, and although one can say with confidence that the effects will lay within certain limits, it is impossible to anticipate precisely what the surface quality will be. This freedom in allowing things to happen is so seductive for the maker and the collector; serendipity, or a happy accident? The unique appeal the raku experience has, in my experience, centres around the particular moment when we open the reduction bin and expose the finished article. But before this opening we hover over the kiln and with anticipation approach the reduction containers. How has the piece reacted to the kiln and reduction, has the glaze worked? These and more questions are asked and finally answered, at the great 'unveiling'.

However, it is also my habit to refire until I am satisfied with the results, a practice that can and often does lead to the complete destruction of the piece. By its very nature, raku leaves an indelible imprint on any work. This can be small crackles in the glaze or glaze that runs; this is not a fault, but as Japanese tradition states, 'The history of the fire'. Moreover, according to Japanese lore, a raku piece that has been given as a gift is very lucky for the owner and should never be given away.

THIS BOOK

Having specialized in raku firing for over twenty years and since having my own web site, I have been inundated with requests for glaze recipes and tips on how to achieve certain types of result. I therefore decided to gather all this information

THIS PAGE:
TOP: **'Shrine'.** *BOTTOM:* **'Shrine' (detail).**
PHOTO: VICTOR FRANCE

OPPOSITE PAGE:
'Shrine No.2'. PHOTO: VICTOR FRANCE

'Temple Tower'.

together in one handbook. The glazes I have collected over these years have come from a number of sources, such as books, journals and the Internet, and, of course, other raku artists, plus some of my own efforts. Several of the glazes I have altered to suit my own style of firing and so they may differ slightly from the original. Where possible I have acknowledged the authors of the glazes, and to the ones I have omitted or have not known I apologize now. Several glazes have been passed around from person to person and the original creator may be forgotten, and in addition the glazes may become changed subtly over time. I hope readers enjoy trying out these recipes and I do stress that everyone should test first before trying out a new glaze on a precious new form or pot. You have to also take into consideration that many ingredients change subtly over time.

This can be observed when a glaze recipe does not produce the same results as before. It also means that you have to retest the glaze recipe with the altered ingredients. Copper and frits are often changed by the manufacturers; frits will be given different ingredients and copper often has 'fillers' added, which can be observed by the colour, as the darker green the copper the more pure copper it contains. Furthermore, reduction has a lot to do with how a raku glaze reacts. A heavy reduction in an airtight container will give an entirely different appearance to the same glaze that has had a very light reduction in an unsealed container. Once again, test with different reduction materials, such as leaves, seaweed (this is best used dry), newspaper (can be useful either wet or dry), pine cones or pine cone needles and different sawdusts such as pine (light wood) or jarrah (dark wood). You can also try a reduction in the kiln during the firing to get different results on your glazes. To me, the joy of raku is in experimenting with all these components and the excitement of opening up the reduction

ABOVE: *'Elegant Lady' (detail)*.
RIGHT: *'Elegant Lady'*.

bin to see what, if anything, you have achieved. You should experiment with all types of glaze, reduction materials, the time of reduction and the oxidation effects. Keep good records of your experiments and in time you will build up a useful source of information. I also multi-fire a lot of my work, anything up to ten times, if I am not happy with it. This can lead to some wonderful results or total destruction; have fun and above all be safe.

In this book I have also invited other raku enthusiasts, people whom I have admired and looked up to, to share my raku journey. They originate from around the world, Australia, Britain, Belgium and the USA. I feel privileged that they took the time and agreed to participate and share their knowledge and experience with us all.

2 RAKU FIRING AND RAKU KILNS

There is an assortment of kilns available for raku, some ready-made and available from your ceramic supplier and others are home-made. Choose the kiln that suits both how you work and the size of your work. I personally have two kilns, a large one and a small one, which is also useful for glaze testing. I do not advocate the use of an electric kiln because the whole raku process is very damaging to the electric elements. Copper too has a detrimental effect on an electric kiln, corroding the elements. A liquid propane gas (LPG)-fuelled, outside kiln, which is movable and very convenient, is also popular, and one I would endorse. If you have natural gas in or near your studio, it can be cheaper to run this type of kiln and you do not have the inconvenience of running out of bottled gas at the wrong moment, but such kilns are usually quite large and not always suitable for use for raku work. You can also build a kiln from bricks and wood fire it. However, I am not going into the construction of kilns here since there are many books available on the subject, one of which is David Jones' *Raku – Investigations into Fire* (Crowood).

If you are new to raku, try to go to some workshops and see as many different kiln types as you can, in that way you will get a good idea as to the

OPPOSITE: **'3 Friars' (multi-fired).**
PHOTO: VICTOR FRANCE

RIGHT: **'Temple' (detail).**

one that would suit you best. The size of a kiln is not the only important factor: there are 'top-hat' kilns or opening door kilns, kilns that are operable by one person or ones that need at least two. Do some research before you commit yourself to one particular type. Firing a kiln is particularly subject to variations, since with most glaze recipes there can be no guarantee of results due to disparities in mixing, firing and sometimes the constituent chemicals. I urge you to always test first, sometimes try to repeat the test under different conditions and reduction atmospheres.

CLAY AND MATERIALS

Almost any kind of clay can be used for raku firing, but the one used most often is one with an open clay body since this helps to give the clay more resistance to the thermal shock of the raku process. If you have a clay body that you like, the addition of grog or other materials should help to give the clay more resilience. Materials such as spodumene or petalite and even washed sand can be useful in this regard, but make sure that these materials are fully wedged throughout the clay. Porcelain can also be used for raku and tends

'2 Friars' (multi-fired copper matt).

not to need any added combustibles, but, due to the low firing temperature, it will not be fully vitrified. Almost all suppliers now have ready-made raku clays available for purchase.

I often like to add other materials to my clay to give some additional texture. Crushed red brick, perlite, fireclay, vermiculite (a lightweight mica-derived mineral), and even copper or brass metal filings may be used. Some types of organic material that burn out but leave a texture can all be utilized in this manner. Experiment with different materials, but do not fire too high since some materials have a habit of exploding, which will not do your kiln much good. I suggest that you first make test tiles with some of the materials you wish to use and test fire them, always keeping records of the amount you used and the temperature you took the kiln to.

FORMS APPROPRIATE FOR RAKU

Some shapes take the thermal shock of raku better than others. Here are a few suggestions that may help in the shaping and forming of your work. Make sure that the work is of an even thickness where possible and not too thick, and try to and make the piece without joints (square boxes are notorious for cracking apart at the seams and flat plates can crack, but if they are curved they tend to be much stronger). Slip-cast pieces are often to be preferred since the thickness of the clay is uniform throughout the whole piece. Attempt to make the piece so that it may easily be picked up with tongs, and make sure that the work will fit into the kiln, not too tall nor too broad. Try the piece first before you glaze it.

'Madonna' (detail of life-size figure).

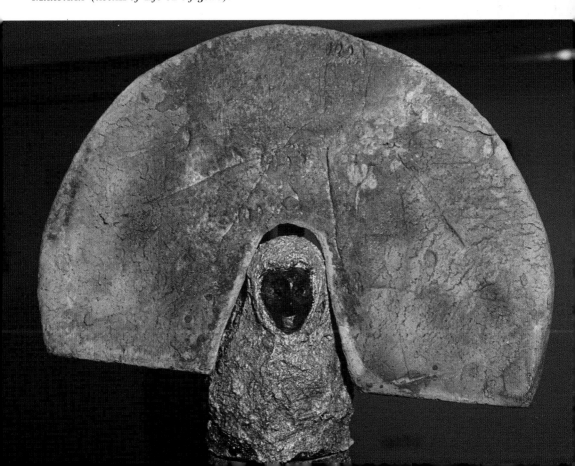

OUTLINE OF A GLAZE COMPOSITION

To help you understand a little about making glazes before you begin, here is a short and simple explanation of their composition. A glaze is made by mixing specific quantities of chemicals and other materials together in water, where they are held in suspension by the viscosity of the liquid blend. Firing the glaze melts this mixture and causes it to fuse permanently on to the surface of the piece. The main components of a glaze are:

- a flux or base; chemical symbol RO; the flux lowers the melting point of a glaze and by the use of more than one flux you can achieve a variation of glaze temperatures;
- a glass stiffener, R_2O_3, usually alumina; the more you use the slower and more viscous the glaze;
- a glass former; RO_2, usually silica; silica has a melting point of $1710°C$ and requires a flux to reduce this to a more workable value;
- colourants and opacifiers; these can often act as fluxes or stiffening agents too;
- alumina is usually added as clay and is used to increase the hardness of the finished glaze and for viscosity during firing.

DECORATION

There are many and varied ways of decorating pieces. Depending on the type of work and the methods used, raku lends itself to many of these diverse methods, apart from using a raku glaze. Raku can also be used in conjunction with other techniques. When making a piece of work it is generally a good idea to have a plan as to the type of decoration you might have in mind, but terra sigillata, resist technique, burnishing and slip are just a few that may be used alone or in conjunction with raku glazes. Textural glazes are excellent when used on a sculptural form and combine quite readily with a resist. A crackle white glaze looks stunning near an area that has been burnished and left to become carbon black. Lustres, slips and oxides can all be applied to raku and will give you a wide range of colours from which to work. The application of a blow-torch may often be used, but I advise you do

'Chalice' (bronze under white crackle).
PHOTO: VICTOR FRANCE

this carefully so as not to heat up one area too much; if you have fired the piece with a copper-based glaze a blowtorch can frequently give you some good results.

During my university studies, a lecturer, Kate Williams, introduced me to a simple but effective idea which works best on a small item or area. Because of the results, Kate called it the lead glass technique; draw your pattern on the bisque ware as you would for a lead glass design. Use a wax resist to outline the design, just like the lead between the glass pieces would look, then fill in the blank areas with stains or oxides, let them dry between each coat and then carefully cover this part with a clear glaze. After raku firing you will see that the black carbon has penetrated only where the wax resist has been, leaving the coloured area free from it.

Paper resist is often used in raku firing since it gives you good clean lines and crisp finishes for glaze and carbon areas. One of the easiest methods is with the use of newspaper or strong tissue paper. Newspaper is thicker and easily obtained, whereas a strong tissue paper is more flexible and easier to bend after wetting. Make sure that whichever paper you use is thoroughly wet so that it has already expanded; if it is not wet enough it will have the tendency to peel at the edges. Paper resist can be used for both slips and glazes. After placing the paper on the piece ensure that you sponge it down thoroughly; this is to make sure that the edges are well and truly stuck down. After the paper has been applied to the piece and sponged, carefully go over it with a drier sponge to take up any excess of moisture and immediately this has been done you should apply the slip or glaze. Once the slip or glaze has dried, taking probably about 30min, carefully remove the paper resist.

Working with clay has been my preferred medium for about the past twenty years and raku is my obsession. At the present, my work is con-

'2 figures' (copper/gold glazes).
PHOTO: VICTOR FRANCE

cerned with ancient monuments that have been lost in time and the elements. Using the clay and glazes to give texture and in some cases adding a copper patina, I find that I am able to represent this time long past. The glazes used took me many months to devise and test until I was happy with the final results. As in all things, to get satisfaction you need to work hard and have patience.

17

3 RAKU TECHNIQUES AND PROBLEMS

GLAZING AND APPLICATION

It is advisable, and a practice which I prefer in order to be on the safe side, to glaze all work the day before you raku, although it is possible to dry the work by sitting it on or near the edge of the hot kiln on the day. This is really only acceptable if you are glazing only small items; wet or damp glazed work will crack or even shatter in the kiln and this can destroy the kiln and make a terrible mess of its shelves.

Glazes may be applied in any manner that you find fits the piece and that you are comfortable using. Pouring, dipping, sponging, painting and spraying are all suitable for a raku glaze. As in all glazed surfaces, ensure that you have sufficient glaze on the work; for instance, a crackle glaze will not crackle if it is too thin, and a matt copper will not present you with the iridescent colours you are seeking if insufficient glaze has been applied (but this glaze in particular often gives you better results if it has only a thin layer, a complex and frustrating 'Catch-22' situation, that, after many trial and error efforts, can be overcome with experience).

CRAZING

Crazing looks like a network of cracks in the glaze. In a normal glaze this would be a defect but in a raku glaze this is often the effect you are looking for. Crazing is caused by a different expansion/contraction between the body and the glaze; in other words, the glaze is actually too small for the body and, when cooling, contracts

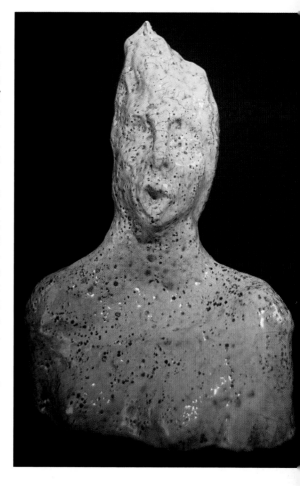

ABOVE: 'Water Nymph' (white crackle, multi-fired).

OPPOSITE: 'Fractured Discourse' (white crackle and shiny black glaze). PHOTO: VICTOR FRANCE

19

more than the body, thus causing the craze effect. When a glaze has been created to obtain this effect it is called a crackle glaze. Depending on the composition of the glaze, you can obtain large or small crackles and often you do not see them until you have warmed the piece again and placed ink over it, which then goes into the crackles; after washing off the piece the cracks are shown up by the ink.

PINHOLING

Pinholing looks as it suggests, like many small pinpricks on the surface of the glaze after the firing. This can occur when a glaze is applied too thinly: insufficient glaze is available to heal over the pinholes in the firing. But if a glaze is too thick you get a much larger bubble and larger pinholes. These holes appears during the fusion process of the firing, the gas bubbles burst during the firing and do not 'heal' over, creating this effect.

Bubbles are created in large numbers in all glazes during the fusion process. Sometimes it is purely contamination of a glaze that generates this fault, therefore always make sure that you practise good housekeeping in your studio and ensure that your bulk liquid glazes are well covered from dust, dirt and any other contamination and that no dried out glaze falls into the mix since this can also contain air bubbles.

CRAWLING AND BEADING

Bare patches on your glazed pieces are often the fault of 'crawling'. This happens when the bisqued work has had dirt, dust, oil or grease inadvertently applied to it. The glaze then rolls away from these areas, acting like a resist. Always keep bisque ware away from any of these contaminants. However, some glazes are prone to crawling due to their high surface tension.

SHIVERING OR PEELING

The opposite of crazing is 'shivering' which is caused by the glaze being too big for the body and thus on cooling the glaze shivers or peels off the body, most often on the edge or rims. What is happening is that the body of the piece is squeezing through the glaze; this is not a very common problem because a glaze can withstand much compression before it will start to shiver.

STARVED GLAZE

You sometimes get a glossy glaze that comes out looking dull and lifeless; this is often called a 'starved glaze'. The cause is quite frequently that of underfiring, and in such a case you can refire the piece to obtain a better result. Too thin an application of glaze may also give the same dull appearance; this may be caused by the use of a spray gun. Sprays can be difficult to use since you can over-glaze one area, while not giving another area enough. A glaze that is mixed with too much water and is thus too thin will give you the same effect. A good rule of thumb for a glaze is that it should be as thick as cream.

DUNTING

If a crack has penetrated completely through the wall of the piece this is called 'dunting' and can be caused by factors such as thermal shock (*see* below) in cooling or heating. In the cooling-down phase a dunt can be identified by its sharp, jagged edges, while a heating dunt will have smooth, rounded edges.

SLUMPING AND WARPING

Overfiring a piece of work will often result in a form's slumping or warping. This is caused by the body being subjected to heat beyond its normal firing range and this in turn causes the fluxes to soften, which results in the body's collapsing.

Often this is caused by placing a large piece of work too close to the heat source, thus it is better to put a tall piece in the centre of the kiln. Badly designed work can also lead to your work's collapsing. If the base of your work is thicker than the walls this can cause uneven heating, which, in turn, causes stress and ultimately the slumping and warping of the piece.

THERMAL SHOCK

Thermal shock is caused by stress within a ceramic object resulting from temperature changes and is the biggest cause of cracks and faults in firings; this can happen with a sudden change in temperature from hot to cold, or the placing of a piece so that one area of it gets a full blast of heat from the kiln while another is shielded by other work

or a kiln prop. The structure of work may also add to thermal shock: having a thick bottom and thinner sides will cause parts of the work to react differently to heating and cooling, often resulting in fractures.

GLAZE FIT

Glaze fit is the suitability of a glaze to fit to the underlying clay body with regard to its thermal expansion and contraction. The body of the work and the glaze need to have the ability to expand and contract together with reasonable harmony. However, an exact match is not possible and fortunately not necessary since there is a degree of latitude before a defect occurs. This is a predicament that can often be fixed by first analysing the problem.

LEFT: 'Le Promenade' (slip and raku hat). PHOTO: VICTOR FRANCE

BELOW: 'Temple Bells' (bronze/beads/copper red glazes).

GLAZE STORAGE

Raku glazes are usually made up as needed since they do not store well and will often settle at the bottom of a container if left for any length of time. If you have made up a large amount of glaze and need to store it, make sure that its container has a tightly fitting lid. I usually re-sieve the whole lot and give it all a good stir to make sure that all the ingredients are thoroughly mixed again. Copper compounds are well-known for settling.

Experiment with other oxides and colourants if you find a base glaze you like. Raku firing is

---

TIPS AND TRICKS IN RAKU

- Over-glaze spray: spray copper oxide thinly over a white crackle then fire and reduce.
- Lustre effects: place copper carbonate in a muslin bag and shake it over a damp piece, causing it to stick on the surface; you can also paint a thin wash of either copper carbonate or copper oxide on to a bisque piece, under a glaze.
- Frit 4108 can often be used in a glaze recipe as a substitute for Gerstley borate, but always test first.
- To a little warm water add 1g of silver nitrate and a pinch of salt; let it dissolve and use over a glaze, for instance, copper red, and then fire as usual.
- When using borax I buy a household brand since it is cheaper and finer; to use it I place the borax and the oxides needed in a separate bowl of hot water to dissolve them; this is then added to the general recipe; by this means the borax does not go hard and lumpy.
- To highlight the cracks in a crackle glaze: warm the piece in the oven after firing, then paint a thin layer of Indian ink over the area of crackle, let it dry and wash under cold water; this closes the cracks over the ink, which then shows up the crackle; this can also be done with stains and other oxides and refired in a normal kiln.
- To get good black carbon make a slip from dry white paperclay and then wash over the selected area; the fibre in the paper seems to pick up the carbon more readily and gives a darker black area from the smoke. The usual black obtained in raku is anything from grey to a smudgy black, this gives a black.
- Saggar firing in a gas kiln: wrap your work in seaweed and tie with string, use shards brushed with copper carbonate/salt/cobalt and then these salt-washed shards are secured under the string; the piece is then placed in a bed of charcoal in a brick box and fired to cone 06 at 1000°C.
- Try using a commercial earthenware glaze (such as Duncan's) in the kiln; you can often get unforeseen results, I have found that the red glazes are usually excellent.
- Cone 6 or less: almost any glaze that has a melting point around 1000°C can be tested in a kiln, but also try stoneware glazes since the result may surprise you.
- Digital thermostat problems: if your digital thermostat starts to give you strange readings it is often an intermittent disconnection and most often in the thermocouple; check the thermocouple circuit, a torch battery and a bulb are as good as any, and then try to trace the break and fix it; if it is in the compensating cable renew it since the cable is relatively cheap; make sure that the cable is connected the right way round.

built on unpredictability and change, so take full advantage of this. Do keep a good record of what you have done since there is nothing worse than getting a fantastic result and then not knowing exactly how you managed to get it. The methods used to apply the glaze can affect the outcome, too. Dipping, pouring, brushing on or spraying are all used and can present you with different colours and effects; the thickness of the glaze is also a factor that can alter the colours.

'Temple'.

TOXIC MATERIALS

Many raku glaze ingredients are toxic and I urge you to take great care in handling and storing these chemicals. Always store away from other chemicals and ensure that they are labelled as toxic. At all times wear gloves and a mask and work in a well-ventilated area. An old bathroom cabinet that can be locked is a useful storage area, especially if is fitted high on a wall.

BODY STAINS AND COLOURANTS

When using body stains or underglaze colours they may end by being very pale. Use 10 per cent or more by weight to the clay to ensure that you get the colour you are looking for; make several 10g balls of the plastic clay and, starting with 1 per cent of the colour add 1 to 2 per cent to each ball, making sure that it is thoroughly mixed into the clay and then test fire. Keep a record of each addition for further use. You might find that some colourants need to be present in much higher concentrations in order to get a discernible colour, but you will learn through testing which ones. Yellow is a good example: I would use a minimum of 5 per cent to start with and go up in increments of 2 or more per cent.

CLEANING

After the pieces have cooled you need to clean any excessive carbon off. Wash the pieces in water, using a brush gently to get to the stubborn carbon; I often use an old toothbrush for difficult areas and you can also use stiff bristle brushes, but carefully, and a good proprietary cleaner is useful, something that you would use to wash pots and pans. Rinse thoroughly to get any residue off and leave to dry.

Raku is fun and exciting but can also be hazardous; I cannot stress enough that safety should be of the utmost importance. This safety advice should be used in addition to all other normal safety precautions that are taken in any ceramic studio.

- When making up glazes always wear an appropriate dust mask and gloves (I find the disposable kind are useful) particularly when using toxic materials; where possible ask your supplier for *Material Safety Data Sheets*; if your supplier does not have these, ask them to get them or go direct to the chemical manufacturer; these sheets are useful as they will usually give you instructions as to how to store the products and information on the hazards they might present.
- Never put bare hands into a bucket of glaze since some materials can be absorbed into the skin.
- Be sure to label hazardous material with correct and legible labels and keep them in a safe and secure manner, for example, silver nitrate should be kept in a dark container and away from any heat source; always wear gloves when handling it and wash hands thoroughly after use, silver nitrate will stain clothing, skin and anything else it touches.
- Ensure that you work in a well ventilated studio or workshop; if possible, have an extractor fan fitted.
- Wear protective clothing while loading or removing the work from the kiln; leather is very good in this respect; long gloves should be used, such as welder's or some that are specially made for hot work; long pants and fully enclosed shoes should always be worn and a welder's helmet with visor and a leather apron are also useful.
- Use welder's goggles to peer into the kiln when judging the 'melt'.
- Use a facemask with filter when making the glazes and using some of the chemicals.
- Use long-handled tongs to handle the work into and out of the kiln to reduction containers.
- Do not touch anything unless you are wearing protective gloves while in the process of raku firing, assume that everything is hot.
- Double check that no reduction material is still burning after your firing has been completed; this particularly applies to sawdust since this can burn quietly away without your noticing.
- Always have water and a fire extinguisher near at hand during a firing.
- Keep gas bottles away from the kiln and always make sure that they have been turned off completely at the end of the day.
- Keep gas burners and bottles in good order and if possible have a cut-off thermocouple on your burner.
- Keep your work area clear: the area you use for firing should be away from any inflammable vegetation and free from any trip hazards.
- During firing and reducing keep non-essential people well away from the kiln; if there is a wind keep such people upwind so that any smoke or fumes are directed away.
- Before leaving the work area ensure that everything is cool and not liable to ignite again; ensure that any hot kiln shelves are cool enough be stored and that the kiln is safe enough to be left.

4 RAKU GLAZES A–Z

GLAZE MAKE-UP RECIPES

Glaze Name	Composition	Weights (g)	Description
Alkaline Blue (needs a heavy reduction to get the copper flashing; use a dark sawdust rather than pine)	frit 4110 silica soda ash Gerstley borate kaolin copper carbonate	70 10 10 5 5 3	a little blue with copper glaze too thin
Alligator #1	Gerstley borate bone ash nepheline-syenite copper carbonate bone ash	50 30 20 1.5 3	crusty matt surface
Alligator #2 (can be dull but looks good adjacent to other glazes, especially on a sculptural piece)	nepheline-syenite copper carbonate cobalt carbonate	2 1.5 ¼tsp	
Alligator #3 (good rusty colour when applied thinly but can lose colour if applied too thickly)	Gerstley borate nepheline-syenite bone ash copper carbonate	40 10 10 10	dry red rust colour, apply thinly
Alligator Crawl	Gerstley borate bone ash nepheline-syenite copper carbonate tin oxide	25 12.5 6.25 6.25 5.35	can be used as a textural glaze
Antique White (creamy white colour)	talc	20	

continued overleaf

OPPOSITE: *'Gates of Heaven' (Black Raku/Mike's Gold).* PHOTO: VICTOR FRANCE

GLAZE MAKE-UP RECIPES *continued*

Glaze Name	Composition	Weights (g)	Description
Apple Crackle (needs to be fired to 1100°C; copper matt glaze on top acts as a reduction to under glaze)	kaolin Gerstley borate red iron oxide	20 80 10	apple crackle on a bisque piece then spray the copper
ADD this copper matt glaze:	copper oxide frit 4101	10 80	matt on top
Base Glaze #1	frit 4101 bentonite whiting ball clay zinc oxide	80 4 8 4 4	good general base for oxide addition
Base Glaze #2	frit 4110 kaolin bentonite	94 5 1	
Base Glaze (Ron Hicks) (good starting point)	Gerstley borate nepheline-syenite	60 40	
ADD:	copper carbonate	3	for colour
Base Glaze 50/50 (basic start to many raku glazes)	Gerstley borate nepheline-syenite	50 50	
Base Glaze (Clear) (Soldner's) (good starting point)	Gerstley borate nepheline-syenite	80 20	
Black (glaze has a broad firing range; useful if you are using other glazes in one firing when you have placed the piece in the reduction bin, allow the flame to lick over the piece before quickly covering it)	Gerstley borate nepheline-syenite barium carbonate lithium carbonate silica kaolin (Edgar Plastic Kaolin) manganese dioxide black copper oxide black iron oxide	45.6 73.8 53.4 29.1 73.8 24.3 30 6 12	

Glaze Name	Composition	Weights (g)	Description
Black (Flat) (glaze has a matt texture and is useful as a foil to white crackle)	Gerstley borate borax iron oxide rutile cobalt carbonate	50 50 10 10 2	matt
Black Raku	borax Gerstley borate soda ash nepheline-syenite ball clay	3.22 43 22 11 22	
Black Widow (can give flashes under heavy reduction)	Gerstley borate nepheline-syenite black copper oxide	80 20 71.7	
Blue (reliable blue glaze)	frit 4110 Gerstley borate silica soda ash china clay	70 5 10 10 5	
Blue Crackle (to get a nice crackle finish, let piece cool slightly before reducing)	Gerstley borate Cornwall stone cobalt carbonate cobalt oxide	80 20 6 7.5	good crackle under reduction
Blue (Dark) Crackle (glaze is almost blue-black)	Gerstley borate nepheline-syenite zirconium silicate kaolin cobalt oxide	70 18 9 5 1.75	
Blue-Dolphin Blue (glaze is a pale crackle blue)	Gerstley borate bone ash nepheline-syenite Cornwall stone copper carbonate cobalt oxide	70 30 20 10 10 0.75	

continued overleaf

GLAZE MAKE-UP RECIPES *continued*

Glaze Name	Composition	Weights (g)	Description
Blue Gloss (Soldner's) (glaze can give good lustre in places, especially if it has been reduced slightly in the kiln)	Gerstley borate nepheline-syenite copper carbonate cobalt oxide	80 20 5 25	lustrous where thick
Blue (Eggshell) (glaze will give a mottled blue to gold under reduction; under heavy reduction can give an orange peel effect)	borax Gerstley borate red iron oxide copper carbonate cobalt	96 96 1 2 3	light blue crackle
Blueberry (glaze can be mottled blue-green, reduce heavily)	Gerstley borate nepheline-syenite zinc oxide cobalt carbonate chrome oxide	80 20 34 17 9	dark blue
Blue Velvet (glaze has a satin velvet sheen, quite dark blue)	frit 4108 nepheline-syenite alumina hydrate titanium oxide cobalt carbonate	65 23 12 10 5	960°C
Blue-Black Lustre (needs heavy reduction but can give a lustrous blue to black)	frit 4101 whiting ball clay zinc oxide cobalt oxide red iron oxide copper carbonate Gerstley borate	80 8 4 4 3 3 4 20	
Blue Lustre #1 (Seth's; like most lustres needs heavy reduction)	nepheline-syenite tin oxide copper carbonate cobalt carbonate	5 0.3 2.5 1.25	

Glaze Name	Composition	Weights (g)	Description
Blue Lustre #2 (lustre with some copper flashing; needs in-kiln and heavy post-firing reduction to get this result)	Gerstley borate borax red iron oxide copper oxide cobalt oxide	50 50 5 5 5	
Blue Lustre #3	borax red iron oxide copper oxide frit 4108 cobalt oxide	50 5 5 30 5	
Blue Grey (glaze can give a mottled blue to grey under reduction) and	spodumene Gerstley borate ball clay red iron oxide cobalt carbonate	35 60 5 1 0.5	
Blue Black Purple (glaze needs in-kiln reduction and heavy post-firing reduction)	Gerstley borate nepheline-syenite copper carbonate rutile	50 50 50 50	silver blue-bronze *continued overleaf*

'Blue Lustre'.

GLAZE MAKE-UP RECIPES *continued*

Glaze Name	Composition	Weights (g)	Description
Blue (in oxidation) (on reduction glaze will give a metal lustre)	sodium bicarbonate	30	
	soda ash	20	
	soda feldspar	60	
	silica	40	
	ball clay	15	
	copper carbonate	4	
Black New Rogers (useful black glaze; goes well with white crackle)	potash feldspar	20	
	Gerstley borate	80	
	red iron oxide	10	
	cobalt carbonate	10	
	black copper oxide	10	
	frit 4110	30	
Black (Chris Thompson's; glaze will still give a black even without manganesedioxide)	nepheline-syenite	20	good black
	Gerstley borate	50	
	manganese dioxide	4.5	
	cobalt oxide	4	
	copper oxide	4.5	
	iron oxide	3.5	
Black Metallic (glaze gives good metal flashes of colour backed with a dark black; in-kiln reduction as well as post-firing is recommended)	Gerstley borate	45.6	heavy reduction
	nepheline-syenite	73.8	
	barium carbonate	53.4	
	lithium carbonate	29.1	
	silica	73.8	
	kaolin	24.3	
	manganese dioxide	30	
	black copper oxide	6	
	black iron oxide	12	
	cobalt carbonate	6	
Bright Blue (glaze is a blue to copper under heavy reduction)	sodium bicarbonate	30	good colour; can give flashes of copper too
	soda ash	20	
	soda feldspar	60	
	silica	40	
	ball clay	15	
	copper carbonate	4	

continued overleaf

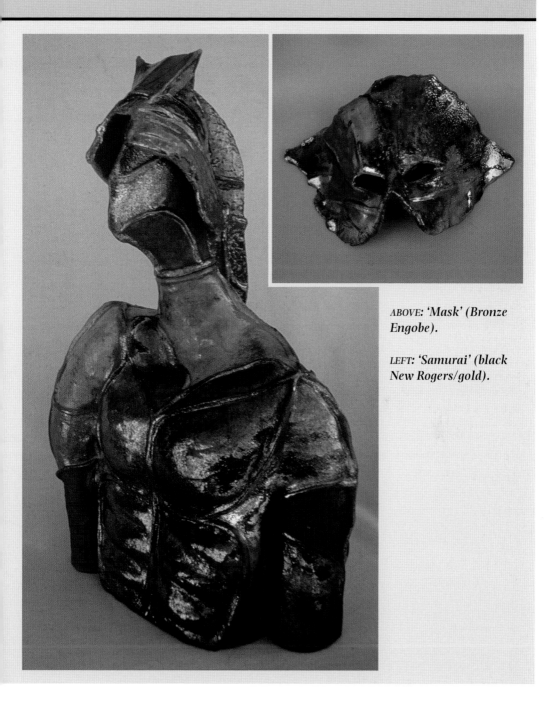

ABOVE: **'Mask'** *(Bronze Engobe).*

LEFT: **'Samurai'** *(black New Rogers/gold).*

GLAZE MAKE-UP RECIPES *continued*

Glaze Name	Composition	Weights (g)	Description
Bronze Engobe (also useful as matt glaze)	copper carbonate	30	good bronze effects
	manganese dioxide	40	
	ball clay	10	
	kaolin	20	
Bronze #1 (glaze will give good lustre colours if blowtorch is used)	black copper oxide	4	960°C, or until shiny
	cobalt oxide	2	
	manganese dioxide	35	
	ball clay	4	
	terracotta (dry clay)	46	
	silica	4	
	red iron oxide	2	
	rutile	3	
	bentonite	3	
Bronze #2	kaolin	30	heavy reduction
	nepheline-syenite	25	
	frit 4110	15	
	manganese dioxide	80	
	copper oxide	30	
Bronze #3 (needs heavy reduction to get colours)	frit 4110	16	
	kaolin	30	
	nepheline-syenite	25	
	lithium carbonate	5	
	copper carbonate	10	
Blue Grey (in-kiln reduction and heavy post-firing reduction)	spodumene	35	
	Gerstley borate	60	
	ball clay	5	
	red iron oxide	1	
	cobalt carbonate	0.5	
Blue (Jack's) (nice blue can give flashes of copper)	Gerstley borate	66	
	nepheline-syenite	25	
	kaolin	5.5	
	borax	4.5	
	copper carbonate	2.5	

'Male Torso'
(blue/copper/
gold).

Glaze Name	Composition	Weights (g)	Description
Blue (Oxidized)	sodium bicarbonate	30	needs no reduction
(plain blue)	soda ash	20	
	soda feldspar	60	
	silica	40	
	ball clay	15	
	copper carbonate	4	
Blue Speckles	Gerstley borate	70	
(mix borate with water	cobalt carbonate	5	
before adding dry			
carbonate; mix only			
small amount since after			
remixing this will have			
no speckles)			
Black Gloss	Gerstley borate	40	
(glaze has a highly	BBR (a ball clay)	20	
glossy sheen under	soda ash	20	
heavy reduction)	nepheline-syenite	10	
	cobalt carbonate	4	
	copper carbonate	2	
	borax	10	*continued overleaf*

GLAZE MAKE-UP RECIPES *continued*

Glaze Name	Composition	Weights (g)	Description
Black (do not over-fire glaze)	bentonite	2	960°C
	frit 4064	40	
	sodium bicarbonate	40	
	silica	20	
	red iron oxide	10	
	cobalt oxide	3	
Bubble Gum Glaze (fire glaze until bubbles clear, around 960–80°C	Gerstley borate	80	satin matt
	potash feldspar	15	grey to blue and
	whiting	5	purple to pink
	zirconium silicate	5	colours produced
	red stain	15%	
	chrome oxide	2	
Burgundy Dry Matt (after heavy reduction will have reddish matt surface)	Gerstley borate	50	
	talc	30	
	nepheline-syenite	20	
	copper carbonate	3	
Burgundy (reduce in-kiln and post-firing)	frit 4064	40	960–80°C
	bicarbonate of soda	40	
	silica	20	
	bentonite	2	
	tin oxide	4	
	manganese dioxide	4	
Chartreuse Green (will give you a yellow-green, needs to be applied thickly)	frit 4110	80	heavy reduction
	tin oxide	4	
	red iron oxide	1	
	potassium bichromate	8	
	bentonite	3	
Cherry Ripe Red	frit 4101	60	
	frit 4110	20	
	kaolin	10	
	tin oxide	4	
	copper carbonate	7	

Glaze Name	Composition	Weights (g)	Description
Clear Glaze #1 (good clear glaze useful on colour stains in raku) on	frit 4108 borax kaolin silica	60 20 10 10	
Clear Glaze #2 (useful base glaze for addition of oxides)	Gerstley borate nepheline-syenite kaolin	70 20 10	good clear glaze
Clear Glaze #3 (good over slips)	frit 4108 borax kaolin silica whiting bone ash copper carbonate	60 20 10 10 1.2 0.8 0.8	
Coffee (light brown, mottled)	Gerstley borate nepheline-syenite rutile	80 20 18	
Coil Water Blue (needs only light reduction)	Gerstley borate silica soda ash kaolin	5 10 10 5	nice crackle blue
Copper (needs heavy reduction, try both in-kiln and post-firing reduction)	copper carbonate frit 4110 kaolin frit 4064 bentonite	80 16 11 3 3	good copper
Copper Iron (greyish black rather than a true dark black)	Gerstley borate nepheline-syenite Cornwall stone yellow ochre copper carbonate	30 10 20 30 10	smooth black

continued overleaf

GLAZE MAKE-UP RECIPES *continued*

Glaze Name	Composition	Weights (g)	Description
Copper Iron smooth matt, dark black (nice matt, dark black)	Gerstley borate nepheline-syenite copper carbonate red iron oxide	30 10 30 30	
Copper Blue #1 (copper flashes under heavy reduction)	frit 4108 nepheline-syenite soda feldspar borax rutile copper carbonate	40 40 14 10 10 3	
Copper Blue #2 (Note: reduce in kiln as well as heavy post-firing reduction)	frit 4110 Gerstley borate silica soda ash kaolin copper carbonate	70 7 10 10 5 3	
Copper Blue/Red #1 (glaze is good with lustre glaze on top, excellent with *Mike's Gold* over)	frit 4108 ball clay zirconium silicate copper carbonate	86 15 15 10	
Copper Blue/Red #2 (try both heavy and light reduction for different effects; takes lustre and gold well)	frit 4108 Gerstley borate silica kaolin copper carbonate bentonite	45 40 7 8 6 3	
Copper Blue-Bronze (glaze has a blue-bronze range; needs to be reduced in kiln and post-firing)	borax Gerstley borate nepheline-syenite potash feldspar copper carbonate	4 42 42 15 4	
Copper Crap (Pattie's) (watch so as not to over-fire)	frit 4112 soda feldspar borax copper carbonate	75 20 5 5	fire until shiny

Glaze Name	Composition	Weights (g)	Description
Copper Matt *(R. Bazemore's)*	copper carbonate frit 3110 bentonite	90 30 3	needs heavy reduction in sawdust
VARIATIONS:			
First	1st layer of copper matt over 2nd layer of mottled brown		gives: reds to oranges
Second	1st layer of mottled brown, 2nd layer of copper matt		gives: strong yellow
Third (use thin layers)	1st layer of Rick's turquoise, 2nd layer of mottled brown, 3rd layer of copper matt		gives: greens, reds, oranges, silver
GLAZE IS GOOD TO EXPERIMENT WITH, TRY ALL VARIATIONS			
Copper Matt (Hasselle's) (has flaky matt texture)	black copper oxide ball clay bentonite Gerstley borate	80 20 2 80	matt
Copper Matt (Hutchins)	nepheline-syenite bone ash cobalt carbonate copper carbonate	20 20 3 7	copper, semi-matt
Copper Matt (excellent, with good colours)	red copper oxide red iron oxide frit 4110 lithium carbonate copper oxide barium carbonate	78.26 8.7 13.4 40 50 10	950–1020°C; heavy reduction; then open reduction bin, let flare then quickly close bin again
Copper Matt #2 (no frit; good results with this: blues, reds, copper)	lithium carbonate copper oxide red copper oxide black barium carbonate	50 25 25 60	heavy reduction

continued overleaf

GLAZE MAKE-UP RECIPES *continued*

ABOVE: **'Blue Flash'**
(Copper Matt glaze).

LEFT: **'Arab' (Copper Matt).**
PHOTO: VICTOR FRANCE

Glaze Name	Composition	Weights (g)	Description
Copper Matt #3	barium carbonate	4.17	900°C
(Leman's)	borax	4.17	
	copper carbonate	62.5	
	lithium carbonate	12.5	
	frit 4108	16.66	
to any copper matt	lithium carbonate	20–35%	for added blues
glaze you can ADD:	barium carbonate	40–60%	and greens
Copper Motown Rust	Gerstley borate	30	dry matt texture
(gives rusty matt	nepheline-syenite	10	
colour)	Cornwall stone	20	
	nickel oxide	20	
	copper carbonate	20	*continued overleaf*

ABOVE: '*Copper Matt #3*'.

FAR LEFT: '*Copper Matt #2*'.

LEFT: '*Pagoda*' (*Copper Matt*).

41

GLAZE MAKE-UP RECIPES *continued*

Glaze Name	Composition	Weights (g)	Description
Copper Lustre #1	frit 4110	74	needs heavy
	nepheline-syenite	11	reduction in dark
	ball clay	5	sawdust
	kaolin	3	
	tin oxide	2	
	copper oxide	10	
Copper Lustre #2	frit 4110	37	needs heavy
	Gerstley borate	37	reduction
	nepheline-syenite	11	
	ball clay	5	
	silica	5	
	kaolin	3	
	tin oxide	2	
	copper oxide	10	
Copper Lustre #3	Gerstley borate	80	no lustre if applied
(Soldner's)	nepheline-syenite	20	too thinly
	cobalt oxide	1	
	yellow ochre	8	
	copper carbonate	2	
Copper Lustre #4	frit 4108	60	dry matt texture
(matt finish, copper	kaolin	30	
sheen)	whiting	10	
	copper oxide	5	
Copper Penny	Gerstley borate	80	very good
(good copper lustre;	potash feldspar	20	
heavy reduction	copper carbonate	2	
needed)	cobalt carbonate	1	
	yellow ochre	7	
Copper Red 1	frit 4108	94	good
(needs heavy	copper oxide	1	
reduction)	bentonite	5	
Copper Red II (Soldner's)	Gerstley borate	80	
(heavy reduction in	nepheline-syenite	20	
kiln and post-firing)	cobalt carbonate	1	
	copper oxide	3	

continued overleaf

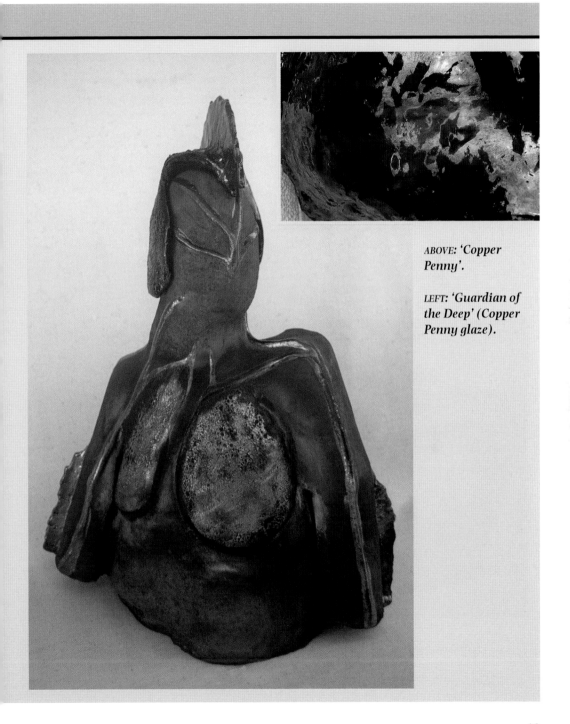

ABOVE: 'Copper Penny'.

LEFT: 'Guardian of the Deep' (Copper Penny glaze).

GLAZE MAKE-UP RECIPES *continued*

Glaze Name	Composition	Weights (g)	Description
Copper Red (Irene's) (heavy reduction)	bone ash	20	gives excellent results with a gold lustre on top of glaze
	Gerstley borate	80	
	tin oxide	1.3	
	copper carbonate	5	
	cobalt oxide	2.5	
Copper Red (Bob's) (heavy reduction)	Gerstley borate	70	
	potash feldspar	30	
	frit 4110	10	
	black copper oxide	8	
Copper Red (Kev's)	frit 4108	90	
	kaolin	10	
	tin oxide	5	
	copper carbonate	1	

ABOVE: *'Male Torso' (Copper glaze).*

RIGHT: *'Entombed' (Crusty Rusty glaze).*

Glaze Name	Composition	Weights (g)	Description
Copper Sand	Gerstley borate	80	matt; nice copper
	bone ash	20	sheen
	copper carbonate	5	
	cobalt carbonate	0.5	
	frit 4110	10	
Cranberry Lustre	Gerstley borate	80	needs heavy
	nepheline-syenite	20	reduction; when
	cobalt carbonate	1.1	applied thinly will
	copper oxide	2.1	give some silver
	yellow ochre	7.8	flashes
Crusty Rusty	colemanite	80	good colour, nice
	bone ash	20	texture; excellent
	copper carbonate	5	with matt glazes
	cobalt oxide	2.5	
Crusty Copper	borax	34	mottled copper;
	Gerstley borate	33	heavy reduction
	kaolin	33	
	copper carbonate	15	
	nickel oxide	10	
Curole Blue	Gerstley borate	50	mostly blue with
	borax	50	some reds; heavy
	cobalt oxide	2	reduction
Curdle Blue	Gerstley borate	50	
	borax	50	
	cobalt carbonate	0.35	
	rutile	3	
Dark Blue (Soldner's)	Gerstley borate	80	lustrous blue with
	nepheline-syenite	20	1–2% silver nitrate
	cobalt carbonate	3	
	iron chromate	5	
	silver nitrate	1.5	

continued overleaf

45

GLAZE MAKE-UP RECIPES *continued*

Glaze Name	Composition	Weights (g)	Description
Dark Blue-Black Velvet	Gerstley borate	30	crusty matt texture,
	nepheline-syenite	10	needs heavy
	alumina oxide	20	reduction
	cobalt oxide	20	
	rutile	20	
Darwin Raku	Gerstley borate	25	
	frit 4108	25	
	tin oxide	2.55	
	copper carbonate	3.25	
Diane's Rainbow	Gerstley borate	30	
(reduce in kiln; post-fire	silica	10	
to achieve colours)	nepheline-syenite	10	
	spodumene	15	
	lithium carbonate	10	
	copper carbonate	3	
Dolphin Clement Blue	Gerstley borate	7	needs heavy
(works better with	bone ash	3	reduction under
synthetic bone ash)	nepheline-syenite	2	sawdust
	Cornwall stone	1	
	copper carbonate	1	
	cobalt oxide	0.75	
Dragonfly	frit 4108	45	matt texture
	Gerstley borate	40	sometimes useful in
	kaolin	8	sculptural pieces
	silica	7	
	copper carbonate	6	
Dry Orange	frit 4064	62	hard to achieve this
	potash feldspar	20	colour, try in-kiln
	barium carbonate	9.9	reduction
	kaolin	42	
	copper carbonate	20	
	tin oxide	10	
	magnesium carbonate	15	
	lithium carbonate	5	

Glaze Name	Composition	Weights (g)	Description
Egyptian Blue	soda ash	30.5	nice, blue, leave to
	lithium carbonate	8.5	cool for a minute
	kaolin	22.5	before placing in
	silica	38.5	reduction
	black copper oxide	2.5	
	bentonite	1	
Egyptian Paste	soda ash	5.89	slip or glaze
	sodium bicarbonate	5.89	
	soda feldspar	38.23	
	ball clay	11.76	
	silica	38.23	
	copper carbonate	29.4	
Emerald-Shiny	frit 4108	90	nice emerald green,
	bentonite	2.5	but get better colour
	ball clay	2.5	if used on terracotta
	kaolin	5	
	tin oxide	5	
	copper carb	8	
Fantasy	Gerstley borate	80	blue with silver
	bone ash	20	flashes in reduction
	tin oxide	1.25	
	cobalt oxide	2.5	
	black copper oxide	5	
Faux Celadon	Gerstley borate	75	green/blue shiny
	kaolin	10	glaze; celadon effect
	silica	15	develops with black
	red iron oxide	2	iron oxide
Flame Drop (A)	magnesium carbonate	40	satin matt
	lithium carbonate	20	
	Gerstley borate	70	
	copper carbonate	6	
	chrome oxide	0.3	
Flame Drop (B)	as above, but with:		
	chrome oxide	3	

continued overleaf

GLAZE MAKE-UP RECIPES *continued*

Glaze Name	Composition	Weights (g)	Description
Fire Flash (Dry)	frit 4110	15	900°C good flash
	frit 4064	4	copper effect
	kaolin	9	
	copper carbonate	72	
Friday Surprise	Gerstley borate	24	heavy reduction for
	nepheline-syenite	60	colour flashes; the
	copper carbonate	1	surprise lies in the
			mixed results from it
Glost Track (Soldner's)	red iron oxide	50	use over a glaze for
	copper carbonate	50	lustre effect
Glass Red I	Gerstley borate	50	good shiny red,
	borax	50	best under heavy
	red copper oxide	10	reduction
	black copper oxide	10	
Glass Red II	Gerstley borate	50	
	borax	50	
	iron oxide	10	
	copper carbonate	5	
Glass Red	Gerstley borate	50	1100°C
	borax	50	
	red copper oxide	10	
	black copper oxide	10	
Grey/Blue	spodumene	35	dark blue, good
	Gerstley borate	60	results with a gold
	ball clay	6	lustre on top
	red iron oxide	1	
	cobalt carbonate	0.5	
Green Lustre #1	Gerstley borate	63	
(needs in-kiln reduction	frit 4112	30	
and heavy post-firing	zirconium silicate	5	
to achieve a lustre)	red copper oxide	2	
	rutile	3	
	bentonite	3	

Glaze Name	Composition	Weights (g)	Description
Green Lustre #2 (needs in-kiln reduction and heavy post-firing to achieve a lustre)	Gerstley borate frit 4108 zirconium silicate red copper oxide rutile	63 30 5 2 3	
Green-Orange	frit 4110 soda ash zirconium silicate copper carbonate chrome oxide	65 10 10 1 0.5	colour ranges through green to orange in reduction
Green-Red	frit 4110 soda ash zirconium silicate copper carbonate	65 10 10 2	light reduction for greens, heavy reduction for red
Grey/Blue	spodumene Gerstley borate ball clay cobalt carbonate red iron oxide	35 60 6 0.5 1	dark blue to grey, takes gold lustre on top well
Green Lustre #1	Gerstley borate frit 4112 zirconium silicate red copper oxide rutile bentonite	63 30 5 2 3 3	in-kiln reduction and heavy post-firing reduction needed to get a lustre
Green Lustre #2	Gerstley borate frit 4108 zirconium silicate red copper oxide rutile	63 30 5 2 3	
Green-Orange	frit 4110 soda ash zirconium silicate copper carbonate chrome oxide	65 10 10 1 0.5	under a heavy reduction this will give mottled green to orange colours

continued overleaf

GLAZE MAKE-UP RECIPES *continued*

Glaze Name	Composition	Weights (g)	Description
Green-Red (make up as much as you need, soda ash tends to settle rock hard)	frit 4110 zirconium silicate soda ash copper carbonate	65 10 10 2	
Green-Maroon Lustre	Gerstley borate nepheline-syenite copper carbonate	80 20 3	mottled green to red, reduce heavily
Green (Lime)	frit 4110 whiting ball clay chrome oxide	100 10 10 5.25	vivid colour
Green-Yellow (do not over-fire)	bentonite frit 4064 sodium bicarbonate silica tin oxide potassium dichromate	3 40 40 20 4 8	960–980°C, mottled colour
Green (Runny)	Gerstley borate borax cobalt carbonate iron oxide rutile	50 50 1 5 5	
Green (Poison Ivy)	Gerstley borate nepheline-syenite chrome oxide green nickel oxide	80 20 8 31.5	
Green Smokey Mountain (reduce in kiln as well as post-firing to get best results)	Gerstley borate nepheline-syenite nickel oxide aluminium oxide	80 20 5 3	
Green Cromalux	Gerstley borate nepheline-syenite aluminium oxide chrome oxide	80 20 17 3.5	

Glaze Name	Composition	Weights (g)	Description
Gun Metal 2 glazes: use glaze (a) with Gerstley borate only and (b) with frit only	Gerstley borate (a) frit 4108 (b) nepheline-syenite copper carbonate red iron oxide	30 30 10 30 30	has some good matt red copper
Hawaiian Blue	bone ash Gerstley borate tin oxide copper carbonate cobalt oxide	20 80 1.3 5 2.5	useful blue glaze with nice crackles
Halo Slip *(Soldner's Bisque)*	Gerstley borate kaolin silica	14 57 29	the original Soldner slip to obtain the 'halo' effect
Hal's Blue (use one coat, when not too thick)	frit 4108 nepheline-syenite soda feldspar copper carbonate rutile borax	40 40 14 3 10 10	
Hine's Patina	Gerstley borate bone ash nepheline-syenite Cornwall stone copper carbonate	50 21.5 14.5 7.2 7.2	apply in a thin coat or paint on two thin ones with a sponge to get a result
Honey	borax ball clay red iron oxide	70 30 3	honey-brown crackle, needs to be like thick cream under good reduction
Honey Yellow	Gerstley borate china clay silica zirconium silicate manganese dioxide	55 30 5 5 1	allow to cool slightly before reduction

continued overleaf

GLAZE MAKE-UP RECIPES *continued*

Glaze Name	Composition	Weights (g)	Description
Irene's Black/Copper (do not take out of the reduction bin too early, allow to cool)	borax	9	takes gold well and has copper flashes under heavy reduction
	Gerstley borate	64	
	spodumene or petalite	27	
	copper carbonate	4.5	
	chrome oxide	0.4	
	manganese carbonate	45.5	
	cobalt oxide	¼tsp	

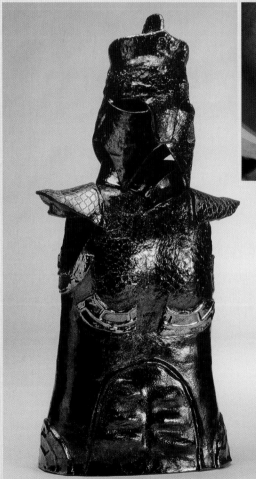

LEFT: *'Legionary' (Irene's Black/Gold lustre).* PHOTO: VICTOR FRANCE

ABOVE: *Irene's Black with Mike's Gold.*

Glaze Name	Composition	Weights (g)	Description
Irene's Red/Bronze Mix	frit 4108	72	red to copper/bronze
	Gerstley borate	25	flashes, sheen
	tin oxide	1.5	
	black copper oxide	5.5	
	bentonite	10	
Iridescent Crater	frit 4108	80	blue, 900°C, silver
	bone ash	20	flashes under heavy
	copper carbonate	5	reduction with some
	cobalt carbonate	3	craters
	bentonite	3	
Iridescent Green (Soldner's)	Gerstley borate	80	good colour, takes
	nepheline-syenite	20	gold lustre well
	copper carbonate	1	
	red copper oxide	1	
	red iron oxide	1	
ADD for more colours:	cobalt carbonate	1	
Iridescent Matt Lustre	Gerstley borate	80	shiny lustre effects
	bone ash	20	when over other
	cobalt carbonate	2.5	shiny raku glazes;
	copper carbonate	5	can be used alone
Iron Yellow (Runny)	Gerstley borate	50	
	borax	40	
	red iron oxide	10	
	rutile	3	
Jade Green	Gerstley borate	23.6	light reduction
	frit 4108	41.6	
	kaolin	34.8	
	tin oxide	5	
	copper carbonate	5	
	bentonite	2	
Jade Green (Soft)	frit 4113	87	lighter than above
	magnesium carbonate	10	
	copper carbonate	3	
	bentonite	3	

continued overleaf

GLAZE MAKE-UP RECIPES *continued*

Glaze Name	Composition	Weights (g)	Description
Kansas	frit 4108	50	matt copper needs
	Gerstley borate	50	heavy in-kiln
	copper carbonate	10	reduction and
	rutile	50	post-firing reduction
Killer Cobalt	Gerstley borate	75	very dark blue/black
(heavy reduction)	nepheline-syenite	25	with copper flashes
	copper carbonate	3	
	cobalt carbonate	6	
	barium carbonate	5	
Lava	kaolin	20	textured glaze
(carefully watch	silica	10	
for bubbling effect,	soda ash	50	
do not over-fire)			
Lettuce and Tomato	frit 4064	64	900°C; reds and
(do not over-fire, this	borax	16	greens
will result in no	spodumene	10	
colours; needs in-kiln	terracotta clay (dry)	10	
reduction and heavy	copper carbonate	5	
post-firing reduction)			
Lemon Lustre (Krysia's)	borax	50	
(used in addition to	frit 4108	50	
a base glaze; then add	base glaze	100	
these ingredients)	manganese dioxide	1.5	
	copper carbonate	3	
Lemon Lustre (Pale)	Gerstley borate	75	
	soda spar	25	
	copper carbonate	3	
	manganese dioxide	1.5	
Lithium Blue #1	Gerstley borate	50	
(heavy reduction	nepheline-syenite	24	
needed)	lithium carbonate	21	
	copper carbonate	2	
	tin oxide	3	

Glaze Name	Composition	Weights (g)	Description
Lithium Blue #2 (reduce in shredded paper to get good lustre red)	lithium carbonate kaolin silica copper oxide bentonite	28 14.5 58 4 3	
Lithium Blue #3 (Matt) (reduce in-kiln; heavy post-firing reduction)	bone ash lithium carbonate whiting kaolin silica copper carbonate bentonite	1.5 28.1 3.5 12.2 55.2 10 3	matt texture can give flashes
Lizard #1 (heavy reduction)	borax spodumene or perlite copper carbonate manganese carbonate chrome oxide	9 64 27 45.5 0.4	some good copper flashes in the black with gold lustre glaze on top
Lizard #2	borax Gerstley borate lithium carbonate magnesium carbonate nepheline-syenite copper carbonate	8 59 13 3 17 3	
Lucy's Lustre (useful lustre, gives copper and deep reds under heavy reduction)	Gerstley borate potash feldspar black copper oxide	60 10 20	reduce in-kiln too
Lustrous Blue (reduce in-kiln plus heavy post-firing reduction)	Gerstley borate potash feldspar zirconium silicate black copper oxide cobalt oxide	80 20 20 40 20	blue-silver lustre

continued overleaf

GLAZE MAKE-UP RECIPES *continued*

Glaze Name	Composition	Weights (g)	Description
Meisel Blue (make sure it is white-hot before removing from kiln)	frit 4110 tin oxide kaolin copper carbonate	100 10 5 1	1001°C; make up as required, stir well before applying; heavy post-firing reduction
Metallic Red (in-kiln reduction as well as heavy post-firing reduction needed)	bentonite frit 4110 Gerstley borate copper carbonate red iron oxide	3 50 50 5 10	good under heavy reduction
Metallic Red #2	borax Gerstley borate copper carbonate red iron oxide	50 50 5 10	
Metallic Red #3	bentonite frit 4110 Gerstley borate copper carbonate red iron oxide	3 50 50 5 10	
Mills Blue (gently swing in the air before placing in the reduction bin)	frit 4112 kaolin cobalt carbonate copper carbonate bentonite	85 15 2 1 2	pale blue crackle
Molly's Copper Matt	bentonite bone ash (synthetic) Gerstley borate frit 4108 nepheline-syenite cobalt carbonate copper carbonate	2 20 50 2.5 10 1.2 10	matt with pinks/reds; works almost every time with shredded paper reduction; increase the colours with additions to the cobalt or add manganese to encourage purples

 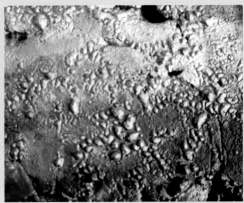

Molly's Copper Matt. *Molly's Copper Matt (thickly applied).*

Glaze Name	Composition	Weights (g)	Description
Mottled Brown (depending on the reduction, glaze will give you varied red-greens to browns)	Gerstley borate nepheline-syenite kaolin copper carbonate red iron oxide	80 20 5 5 10	
Moon	magnesium carbonate kaolin lithium carbonate borax Gerstley borate copper carbonate	50 20 10 40 20 10	very dull matt glaze with a crater/lava finish
Mystery Red Matt	frit 4110 black copper oxide copper carbonate	15 45 45	lovely red matt, often with a crusting texture (a favourite glaze)
Oil Lustre	frit 4108 Gerstley borate copper oxide manganese carbonate	50 50 4.3 1.7	matt/shiny lustre under reduction, but better if you reduce in the kiln too

continued overleaf

GLAZE MAKE-UP RECIPES *continued*

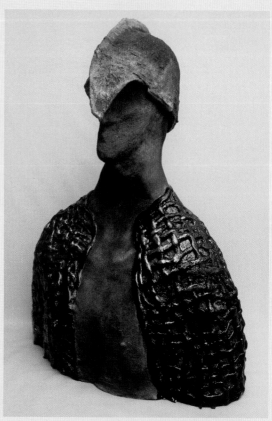

Untitled (Mystery glaze and gold).   *'Rainbow Warrior' (multi-fired).*

Glaze Name	Composition	Weights (g)	Description
Ocean Oil	kaolin	10	heavy reduction
	lithium carbonate	30	
	borax	20	
Pack Man Raku	bone ash	10	satin matt red lustre;
	Gerstley borate	50	good when reduced
	nepheline-syenite	10	in kiln and under
	copper carbonate	10	heavy post-firing
	red iron oxide	1	

Glaze Name	Composition	Weights (g)	Description
Patina (J.Q.'s)	Gerstley borate	80	
	bone ash	20	
	copper carbonate	10	
	tin oxide	1.25	
	cobalt carbonate	0.25	
Patina (Piepenburg's)	Gerstley borate	40	to get a blue patina
	bone ash	30	decrease the
	nepheline-syenite	20	amount of
	copper carbonate	10	carbonate to 2%
Persian Blue	frit 4110	80	needs heavy in-kiln
	whiting	10	reduction and
	ball clay	10	post-firing reduction
	copper oxide	3	in sawdust
	titanium dioxide	4	
	frit 4110	90	
	kaolin	30	
Pinks	red iron oxide	2	needs to be added
	copper carbonate	2	to a base glaze to
			give pinks
Purple (Dark)	red iron oxide	80	almost gloss black
(Mecham's)	copper carbonate	20	
	manganese dioxide	4	
	cobalt oxide	1	
Purple Water	frit 4110	70	
(depending on the	Gerstley borate	5	
colour you are after,	silica	10	
test the manganese	soda ash	10	
at a low level and	kaolin	5	
gradually increase)	add manganese	2–4%	
Purple #1	spodumene	35	
	Gerstley borate	60	
	ball clay	5	
	manganese carbonate	3	
	tin oxide	5	
	black manganese	¼tsp	flat teaspoonful

continued overleaf

GLAZE MAKE-UP RECIPES *continued*

Glaze Name	Composition	Weights (g)	Description
Purple #2	bentonite	2	
	frit 4064	40	
	sodium bicarbonate	40	
	silica	20	
	tin oxide	4	
	manganese dioxide	4	
Purple #3	frit 4108	40	
	Gerstley borate	40	
	borax	10	
	silica	10	
	manganese dioxide	2	
	cobalt oxide	0.5	
Purple #4 (do not over-fire; light reduction)	bentonite	4	960°C
	frit 4101	80	
	whiting	8	
	ball clay	4	
	zinc oxide	4	
	manganese dioxide	2	
	cobalt carbonate	0.5	
Raccoon Copper	potash feldspar	12	
	Gerstley borate	63	
	silica (200 mesh)	12	
	ball clay	6	
	barium carbonate	6	
	copper carbonate	12	
Red Lustre (needs in-kiln reduction and post-firing reduction)	borax	50	bright, glossy glaze
	Gerstley borate	50	
	silica	17	
	nepheline-syenite	15	
	red copper oxide	10	
	red iron oxide	10	
Red Bronze (post-firing heavy reduction will produce good reds/pinks/copper flashes)	frit 4108	50	
	Gerstley borate	50	
	tin oxide	3	
	black copper oxide	2.5	

continued overleaf

'Temple Shrine'
(Copper Red/
Red Bronze).

GLAZE MAKE-UP RECIPES *continued*

Glaze Name	Composition	Weights (g)	Description
Rick's Blue/Gold Over	nepheline-syenite	19.83	needs heavy
	spodumene	20.22	reduction but good
	lithium carbonate	20.62	colour with some
	zirconium silicate	19.11	copper flashing
	copper carbonate	1.29	
	cobalt carbonate	1.29	
Rick's Blue	Gerstley borate	39.3	satin matt; glaze will
	nepheline-syenite	19.83	give copper 'spots' if
	spodumene	20.22	reduced in shredded
	lithium carbonate	20.62	paper
	zirconium silicate	19.11	
	copper carbonate	1.29	
	cobalt carbonate	1.29	
Rick's Turquoise	Gerstley borate	40	nice colour, can
(mix magnesium	nepheline-syenite	19.83	flash in heavy
sulphate with 100ml	spodumene	20.22	reduction
hot water before	lithium carbonate	20.62	
adding)	zirconium silicate	19.11	
	copper carbonate	2.59	
	magnesium sulphate	0.61	
Red/Black/Blue #1	Gerstley borate	70	shiny, heavy
(Lubbuck's)	ball clay	30	reduction to
	tin oxide	1.5	obtain copper
	black copper oxide	5	flashing
Red/Black/Blue #2	Gerstley borate	70	metallic silver with
	ball clay	30	all the colours under
	tin oxide	1.5	heavy reduction
	copper carbonate	5	flashing
Red Bronze	frit 4108	50	good lustre
	Gerstley borate	50	
	tin oxide	3	
	black copper oxide	2.5	

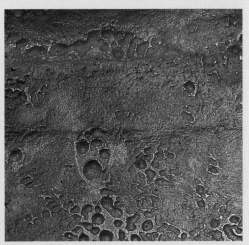

ABOVE: *'Red Lustre'.*

LEFT: *Red/Black/Blue.*

Glaze Name	Composition	Weights (g)	Description
Red Lustre #2	borax	50	lustre reds
	Gerstley borate	50	
	silica	17	
	nepheline-syenite	15	
	red copper oxide	10	
	red iron oxide	10	
Rainbow Copper	borax	70	gold lustre using
	ball clay	30	shredded paper
	copper carbonate	2	
	bentonite	5	
Rainbow (in-kiln reduction and heavy post-firing)	frit 4101	90	
	ball clay	10	
	copper oxide	2	
	tin oxide	2	
	red iron oxide	4	

continued overleaf

GLAZE MAKE-UP RECIPES *continued*

Glaze Name	Composition	Weights (g)	Description
Rainbow Peacock	Gerstley borate	40	can add 10%
	nepheline-syenite	13	spodumene;
	silica	13	turquoise crackle
	lithium	13	with copper flashes;
	copper carbonate	3	heavy reduction
Red Gold	Gerstley borate	80	
(needs in-kiln reduction	or frit 4112	80	
and post-fire reduction	potash feldspar	20	
to get gold/reds)	copper carbonate	3	
Red Bronze	frit 4108	50	can use either red or
	Gerstley borate	50	black copper oxide
	tin oxide	3	
	black copper oxide	2.5	
	or red copper oxide	4.3	
Red Copper 1	frit 4108	40	
	frit 4110	40	
	china clay	10	
	borax	10	
	copper oxide	4	
	tin oxide	5	
Red Copper 2	frit 4108	94	
	copper oxide	5	
	bentonite	1	
Red Hot	nepheline-syenite	50	glaze has an almost
	frit 4108	30	matt texture and
	tin oxide	4	dull red colour
	black copper oxide	1	
Red Bronze Lustre	frit 4108	50	good red/bronze
	Gerstley borate	50	under heavy
	tin oxide	3	reduction, every time
	black copper oxide	2.5	
Raku Red #1	borax	50	
	Gerstley borate	50	
	copper carbonate	10	
	rutile	50	*continued overleaf*

RIGHT: '*Red Gold*'.

BELOW: '*Temple Ruin*'
(*Red Bronze Lustre*).

GLAZE MAKE-UP RECIPES *continued*

Glaze Name	Composition	Weights (g)	Description
Raku Red #2	bentonite	3	
	frit 4110	50	
	Gerstley borate	50	
	copper carbonate	10	
	rutile	50	
Raku Red #3	frit 4112	50	
	Gerstley borate	50	
	copper carbonate	5	
	rutile	50	
Reynolds Rap (use thickly)	frit 4112	63	greens to gold under heavy post-firing reduction
	potash feldspar	12	
	silica	12	
	ball clay	6	
	barium carbonate	6	
	copper carbonate	12	
Special Rainbow (fire as usual to 1000°C, allow kiln to cool to 650°C before removing; best reduced in shredded paper before removal from reduction bin)	copper carbonate	80	matt copper
	frit 4110	15	
	barium carbonate	15	
	lithium carbonate	15	
	magnesium carbonate	15	
	bentonite	5	
Silver Blue-Bronze (in-kiln reduction helps to achieve copper and silver-bronze colours)	Gerstley borate	50	semi-matt with copper flashes
	nepheline-syenite	50	
	copper carbonate	50	
	rutile	50	
Surprise Purple (reduce in newspaper, leave in reduction bin until cool enough to touch)	ferro frit 3110	10	matt with a little colour
	copper carbonate	60	
	red iron oxide	6.75	
	cobalt oxide	3.35	

Glaze Name	Composition	Weights (g)	Description
Soda Blue (allow to cool slightly before reduction to achieve good crackle)	frit 4110	70	crackle
	Gerstley borate	50	
	silica	10	
	soda ash	10	
	kaolin	5	
	copper carbonate	5	
Tan	frit 4108	30	
	Gerstley borate	60	
	tin oxide	2	
	copper carbonate	1	
	rutile	7	
	nepheline-syenite	10	
Tear Drops	Gerstley borate	80	
	nepheline-syenite	20	
	soda ash	6.7	
	cobalt carbonate	9.2	
	cryolite	8.1	
Tin Can (consistency of watered milk)	Gerstley borate	4	metallic patina; can be used on top of others for lustre effect
	nepheline-syenite	3	
	copper carbonate	1	
	black nickel oxide	0.25	
Tomat's Red	borax	50	dull red, can be mottled
	Gerstley borate	50	
	copper carbonate	40	
	red iron oxide	10	
Tsuya's Mistake	copper carbonate	50	can be used on top of other glazes
	frit 4110	50	
Turquoise #1 (apply thickly, heavy reduction in dark sawdust)	bentonite	3	960–1020°C
	frit 4108	90	
	ball clay	2.5	
	kaolin	5	
	copper carbonate	2	
	tin oxide	5	

continued overleaf

GLAZE MAKE-UP RECIPES *continued*

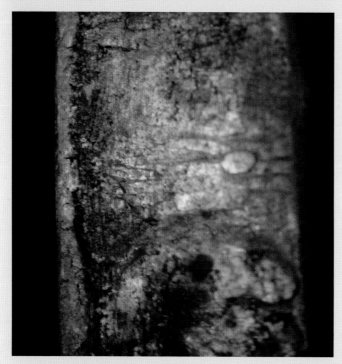

LEFT: 'Tin Can'.

BELOW: 'Turquoise'.

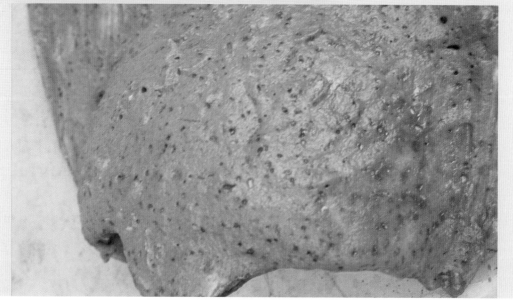

Glaze Name	Composition	Weights (g)	Description
Turquoise #2	frit 4110	70	very good; nice
	soda ash	20	turquoise crackle
	silica	10	with copper flashes
	copper carbonate	4	under reduction
	bentonite	3	
Turquoise #3	frit 4110	70	
	soda ash	20	
	silica	10	
	copper carbonate	4	
	bentonite	3	
Turquoise #4	bentonite	2.5	960–1020°C; good
	frit 4108	90	firing range, useful
	ball clay	2.5	if firing with other
	kaolin	5	glazes
	copper carbonate	2	
	tin oxide	5	
Turquoise #5	frit 4110	40	
	silica	20	
	bicarbonate soda	40	
	copper carbonate	2	
Turquoise #6	frit 4110	80	
	nepheline-syenite	20	
	ball clay	5	
	copper carbonate	5	
	bentonite	3	
Turquoise (Rick's)	Gerstley borate	39.33	very good colour
(add 100ml hot water	nepheline-syenite	19.83	and copper flashes
to magnesium	spodumene	20.22	under heavy sawdust
sulphate before	lithium carbonate	20.62	reduction
adding)	zirconium silicate	19.11	
	copper carbonate	2.59	
	magnesium sulphate	0.61	
Turquoise Crackle #1	Gerstley borate	80	nice crackle glaze
	potash feldspar	20	
	copper carbonate	4	

continued overleaf

GLAZE MAKE-UP RECIPES *continued*

THIS PAGE:
'Ceramic Figure'.
PHOTO: VICTOR FRANCE

OPPOSITE PAGE:
'Rick's Turquoise'.

Glaze Name	Composition	Weights (g)	Description
Turquoise Crackle #2	whiting	80	
	ball clay	40	
	zinc oxide	40	
	bentonite	10	
	zirconium silicate	80	
	copper carbonate	10	
Turquoise Glossy	frit 4110	47	crackle
Crackle (needs only	frit 3124	29	
slight reduction; wave	lithium carbonate	12	
lightly in air before	silica	10	
placing in reduction	bentonite	2	
bin)	copper carbonate	4	

continued overleaf

GLAZE MAKE-UP RECIPES *continued*

Glaze Name	Composition	Weights (g)	Description
Turquoise Love	frit 4110	42.5	heavy reduction
	frit 4108	27.5	for copper flashes/
	lithium carbonate	9.8	green/yellows
	kaolin	6.3	
	silica	14	
	bentonite	2	
	copper carbonate	4.5	
Turquoise Lustre #1	whiting	80	
	ball clay	40	
	zinc oxide	40	
	bentonite	10	
	copper carbonate	2.5	
Turquoise Lustre #2	frit 4110	100	lustre
(Susan Winthrop's)	copper carbonate	3	
	bentonite	2	
	tin oxide	3	
Turquoise (Pale)	Gerstley borate	25	very pale colour
	Cornwall stone	75	that can be lightly
	cobalt oxide	0.1	reduced
	copper carbonate	3	
Turquoise Matt	nepheline-syenite	55	has dry matt texture
	barium carbonate	26	when oxidized; under
	lithium carbonate	2	reduction yellow,
	silica	7	burgundy and black
	china clay	6	produced
	copper carbonate	4	
Tutti Frutti	Gerstley borate	80	good colours,
(heavy reduction)	nepheline-syenite	10	mixture of reds and
	talc	10	coppers and a little
	copper carbonate	5	blue with copper
	bentonite	2	

Glaze Name	Composition	Weights (g)	Description
Vertacnc's Alkaline Blue	frit 4110	70	good blue, copper
	silica	10	flashes; needs a
	soda feldspar	10	heavy reduction
	Gerstley borate	5	
	kaolin	5	
	copper carbonate	3	
Water Blue	frit 4110	70	nice blue crackle;
	Gerstley borate	5	can get reds under
	silica	5	heavy reduction
	soda ash	10	
	kaolin	5	
	copper carbonate	3	
White Raku	frit 4112	40	good white
	frit 4110	40	
	kaolin	15	
	tin oxide	5	
White Crackle (Basic)	Gerstley borate	65	Branfman's favourite
	Tennessee ball clay	5	and most reliable
	nepheline-syenite	15	white crackle
	silica (or flint)	5	
	tin oxide	12	
White Crackle III	frit 4101	80	fine crackles, good
	kaolin	15	on small items
	tin oxide	5	
White (Fat) Crackle	frit 4108	9	
	ball clay	9	
	zirconium silicate	3	
White (Fat) #2	Gerstley borate	30	good larger crackle
	potash feldspar	18	glaze; let cool lightly
	frit 4108	7.2	before reduction
	china clay	1.2	
	tin oxide	3	
	zirconium silicate	0.6	

continued overleaf

GLAZE MAKE-UP RECIPES *continued*

Glaze Name	Composition	Weights (g)	Description
White Matt	frit 4113	87	plain matt, few
	magnesium carbonate	10	crackles
	bentonite	3	
White	frit 4108	90	smooth, glossy
	nepheline-syenite	10	glaze
	ball clay	5	
	tin oxide	10	
add to above glaze recipe for a lustre effect of the white glaze:	frit 4108	20	apply thinly
	borax	10	
	kaolin	50	
	silica	20	
	copper carbonate	4	
White Crackle	frit 4110	47	glossy finish and
	frit 3124	29	nice crackle; needs
	lithium carbonate	12	to cool slightly for
	silica	10	good result
	bentonite	2	
White #1	feldspar	10	
	frit 4108	60	
	silica	10	
	borax	30	
White #2 (Higby's)	silica	10	
	kaolin	20	
	Gerstley borate	30	
White #3	frit 4110	90	
	pot feldspar	10	
	ball clay	5	
White #4 (Roger's)	spodumene	35	
	frit 4112	40	needs to be thick
	ball clay	5	
	tin oxide	5	
for purple add:	manganese carbonate	3	

continued overleaf

'Chinese Figure'
(White Crackle
and Roger's
Black).
PHOTO: VICTOR FRANCE

GLAZE MAKE-UP RECIPES *continued*

Glaze Name	Composition	Weights (g)	Description
Wood Ash Crackle	Gerstley borate	45	blue/copper glossy;
	wood ash	35	depends on type
	silica	15	of ash used
	zinc oxide	5	
Yellow Crackle	Gerstley borate	80	test for amount
(apply thickly for	Cornwall stone	20	of vanadium needed
good results)	vanadium	3–6%	
Yellow Lustre Pale	frit 4112	75	
(under reduction)	soda feldspar	25	
	copper carbonate	3	
	manganese dioxide	1.5	
Yellow	Gerstley borate	80	yellows/green/
(heavy reduction	Cornwall stone	20	rainbow
for colours)	vanadium	3–6%	
Yukio's Rainbow Sand	bone ash	20	
(do not apply too	nepheline-syenite	10	
thickly, to avoid scaly	lithium carbonate	3	
appearance)	copper carbonate	5	
	cobalt carbonate	0.5	
Zowie	Gerstley borate	80	
(depending on the	nepheline-syenite	20	
reduction, glaze can	lithium carbonate	10	
give good copper/red	copper carbonate	5	
flashes; reduce in-kiln	red iron oxide	1	
as well post-firing			
reduction)			

FRITS

A frit is a type of ceramic glass. It is a combination of materials that are melted together to render them insoluble and resistant to acid attack. They are therefore a means of introducing certain materials into a glaze that would otherwise be toxic. Frits can be used alone as low temperature glazes, as in raku and majolica, but generally they form the basis of a glaze recipe.

Lead Frits

Glazes based on lead frits produce a shiny, durable finish and give brightness and clarity of colour when used in conjunction with oxides, stains and slips. While they can be used on all earthenware clays, they are particularly suitable for red clay.

Borax Frits

Borax frits are often used in the production of earthenware glazes when a lead-free glaze is required. A slight milkiness, especially at low temperatures, may be evident over red clays, and the colour response with oxides, for instance, is not usually as vivid as with lead frits.

Alkaline Frits

As with borax frits, alkaline frits are noted for their high soda and potash content. The colour response from copper and manganese is turquoise and purple/brown, respectively – typical of this type of frit. Alkaline frits have a high expansion rate which makes them a suitable base for crackle glazes.

GUIDE TO FRITS

Product Code	Description	Use
DA4193 (replaces F938)	clear, hard, barium borosilicate frit; earthenware 1040–1100°C	not for underglaze colours
DA4110 (replaces F3110, 1078)	leadless, soft, sodium borosilicate frit; earthenware 1000–1060°C	copper-blue and manganese-purple glazes
DA4124 (replaces F3124)	leadless, calcium borosilicate frit; earthenware 1040–1100°C	
DA4171 (replaces F3271, 1057)	leadless, calcium borosilicate frit; earthenware 1040–1100°C	
DA9146 (replaces 9102, 3302D, 1085)	dense zircon white leadless frit; earthenware 1040–1100°C	earthenware white sand pastel-coloured glazes
DA4064 (replaces F4364)	lead bisilicate frit; standard low solubility; earthenware 950–1080°C	
DA4108 (replaces F4508, 3134, 1077)	leadless calcium borosilicate frit; earthenware 1040–1100°C	special effects for raku glazes
DA4113 (replaces F4712)	hard, leadless, clear borosilicate frit; earthenware 1040–1100°C	general purpose for developing colours
DA4194 (replaces F5325P, 501E34, 5301, 1012)	leadless, soft, sodium borosilicate frit; earthenware 900–1060°C	raku glazes

5 ALTERNATIVE METHODS AND MATERIALS OF DECORATION

TEXTURED SCULPTURE GLAZES

Glazes go through a bubbling and boiling process during the course of their firing. Under normal conditions, this bubbling is allowed to progress to its conclusion and eventually subsides. In a crater or lava glaze this is done to obtain a decorative effect. This is achieved by stopping the normal subsidence of these bubbles by removing the glazed piece from the kiln and immediately cooling it, this ensures that these craters become permanently set into the surface of the glaze. As with many raku glazes, the results can be unpredictable and sometimes the edges of the craters are sharp. If this occurs, gently smooth off the sharp sections so that you do not cut yourself when cleaning the piece. I use these glazes on many of my pieces as I do sculptural work, the thickness of the glaze and the firing, as well as the type of reduction all have a bearing on the results obtained. Test the glaze until you get the results you are after (proportions are by weight).

LUSTRES AND SOLUBLE SALTS

Metal chlorides and nitrates are the chemicals most often used to produce lustrous surfaces in a raku glaze. The most common of these are

OPPOSITE: 'Turban Figure' (raku lustre).
PHOTO: VICTOR FRANCE

silver nitrate, bismuth subnitrate and soda ash. These chemicals form a thin metal layer on the surface of the glaze. Gold, silver and iridescent blue are produced under a heavy reduction. These chemicals are frequently expensive and, luckily, you usually need to use only small quantities. I advise making up only as much as you need for each session; silver nitrate is light sensitive and can spoil easily. Glaze the pieces with the lustre just before firing. Keep the unused portion in a dark container that is tightly lidded and always wear gloves as it can also stain your hands.

ENAMELS AND COMMERCIAL LUSTRES

The maturing range of these commercial enamels and lustres are below most raku glaze temperatures and are therefore quite suitable for use over a raku glaze. These on-glaze enamels are really low-temperature glazes, and for most the temperatures at which they can be used is up to 740°C; this is enough to allow them to melt into the glaze and form a bond. Often purchased as powders and mixed with water or turpentine, they are also available ready-to-use and can be placed on the glazed piece direct. They will need several layers to gain the sought-after metallic surface. It is also possible to coat a burnished work to give it a highly lustrous finish.

TEXTURED SCULPTURE GLAZE RECIPES

Glaze Name	Composition	Weights (g)	Description
Beads–Matt	magnesium carbonate	50	white in colour
(glaze looks like beads)	borax	40	
	Gerstley borate	50	
	silica	10	
	zirconium silicate	10	
Craters	magnesium carbonate	20	as name suggests,
(matt texture; watch	kaolin	20	glaze gives a crater
bubbling, carefully, do	lithium carbonate	60	effect
not over-fire)	borax	30	
	copper carbonate	12	
	silica	60	
	bentonite	10	
Earthmother #1	bentonite	10	
(matt texture; glaze	ball clay	10	
has satin matt texture	silica	20	
and gunmetal colour)	talc	10	
	lithium carbonate	30	
	copper carbonate	3	
	cobalt carbonate	1	
	manganese dioxide	3	

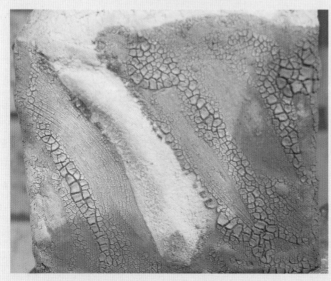

Lava/white.

Glaze Name	Composition	Weights (g)	Description
Lava (glaze needs to be applied quite thickly)	kaolin silica soda ash copper carbonate	20 10 50 10	lava-like appearance
Lichen (slightly green, reduce in kiln as well as post-firing reduction)	frit 3110 black copper oxide red iron oxide	10 40 2.5	mossy texture
Mr King's Raku Glaze (glaze has dry, aged, cracked earth appearance; good for sculptural work; needs to be applied thickly)	frit 4110 black copper oxide red iron oxide Gerstley borate	90 40 2.5 1	matt/dry
Tectonic Plate (to give this glaze a metallic bronze look, add a layer of copper carbonate on top before firing)	Gerstley borate lithium carbonate cryolite zirconium silicate spodumene rutile copper carbonate	20 30 10 25 15 8 1	crusty, dry

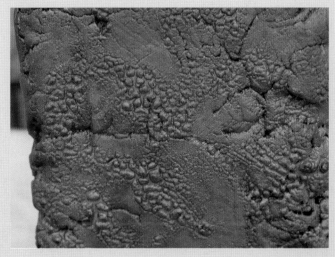

Tectonic Plate.

LUSTRES AND SOLUBLE SALTS RECIPES

Glaze Name	Composition	Weights (g)	Description
Gold Lustre Matt	Gerstley borate	80	
	nepheline-syenite	20	
	silver nitrate	2	
Gold Lustre Gloss	Gerstley borate	80	
	nepheline-syenite	20	
	borax	10	
	silver nitrate	2	
Gold Lustre 11	frit 4101	80	
	whiting	8	
	ball clay	4	
	zinc oxide	4	
	bentonite	4	
	bismuth subnitrate	1	
	silver nitrate	2	
	soda ash	1	
Iridescent Gold Lustre	soda ash	44.2	
	frit 4110	30.9	
	borax	18.6	
	kaolin	24	
	silica	65	
	silver nitrate	1	
	bismuth subnitrate	1	
Gold Iridescence	bismuth subnitrate	10	
	frit 4110	5	
Gold-Silver	Gerstley borate	80	
	Cornwall stone	20	
	tin oxide	1	
	silver nitrate	2	
Blue-Silver	Gerstley borate	80	
	nepheline-syenite	20	nice blue/silver
	kaolin	5	
	tin oxide	1	
	rutile	3	
	cobalt carbonate	1	
	silver nitrate	1	

'Ship of Dreams' (gold lustre). PHOTO: VICTOR FRANCE

Glaze Name	Composition	Weights (g)	Description
Blue-Green-Silver	Gerstley borate	80	nice blue/green
	nepheline-syenite	20	
	kaolin	5	
	tin oxide	1	
	copper carbonate	3	
	antimony oxide	3	
Silver Lustre #1	silver nitrate	2	
	soda ash	1	
Silver Lustre #2	silver nitrate	2	
	soda ash	1	
	chrome oxide	1	*continued overleaf*

LUSTRES AND SOLUBLE SALTS RECIPES *continued*

Glaze Name	Composition	Weights (g)	Description
Silver Lustre #3	silver nitrate	2	
	soda ash	1	
	cobalt oxide	1	
Silver White	Gerstley borate	80	very useful lustre as
	nepheline-syenite	20	it can also be used
	kaolin	5	over other glazes
	tin oxide	1	
	silver nitrate	1.5	
Mike's Gold/Irene's Black Lustre	Gerstley borate	56	
	nepheline-syenite	22.6	
	kaolin	18	
	silver nitrate	3.5	

'Gate of Dreams'.

Glaze Name	Composition	Weights (g)	Description
Hal's Oil Lustre	frit 4108	50	
	Gerstley borate	50	
	copper oxide	4.3	
	manganese carbonate	1.7	
Oil Lustre	bentonite	3	
	frit 112 kmp	70	
	Gerstley borate	30	
	red copper oxide	4.3	
	manganese carbonate	1.7	
Metal Lustre	sodium bicarbonate	30	
(heavy reduction)	soda ash	20	
	soda feldspar	60	
	silica	40	
	ball clay	15	
	copper carbonate	4	
Del Favero Lustre	Gerstley borate	80	
	Cornwall stone	20	
	copper carbonate	2	
Copper Lustre	red copper oxide	2	
(good over other glazes)	bismuth subnitrate	2	
Mike's Gold	bentonite	5	works every time;
Mike Kusnik's	frit 4112	40	excellent results
	frit 4110	47	
	tin oxide	2	
	silver nitrate	6	
Satin Matt Lustre	Gerstley borate	45	quick; heavy
	nepheline-syenite	11	reduction from the
	china clay	16.5	kiln required to get
	borax	27.5	right effects
	copper carbonate	10	
Gold/Silver Gloss	frit 4108	90	
	kaolin	10	
	tin oxide	3	
	silver nitrate	1	

continued overleaf

LUSTRES AND SOLUBLE SALTS RECIPES *continued*

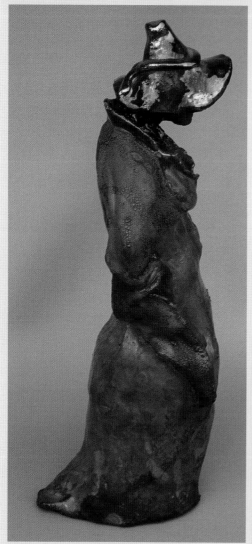

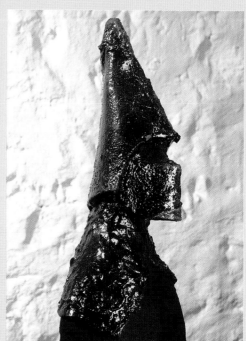

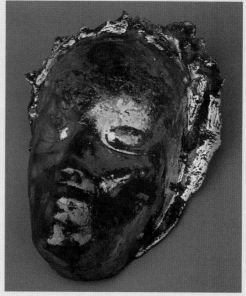

ABOVE: **'Enigmatic Lady' (Copper Matt/Gold Lustre).**
ABOVE RIGHT: **'Wiz' (detail; lustre glaze).**
PHOTO: VICTOR FRANCE
RIGHT: **'Mask' (lustre).**

Glaze Name	Composition	Weights (g)	Description
Gold (Piepenburg's)	Gerstley borate	80	
	Cornwall stone	20	
	tin oxide	1	
	silver nitrate	2	
Raku Lustre	Gerstley borate	80	
	Cornwall stone	20	
	copper carbonate	2	
Net Lustre	Gerstley borate	75	very glossy, blue
	soda feldspar	18	lustre
	zirconium silicate	7	
	cobalt carbonate	4	
	black copper oxide	4	
Seth's Lustre	frit 4112	40	
	bone ash	10	
	copper carbonate	5	
	cobalt carbonate	2.5	
Red Lustre #1	frit 4112	38	
	frit 4108	31	
	frit 4193	31	
	copper carbonate	10	
	iron oxide	10	
Red Lustre #2	frit 4112	38	
	borax	28	
	silica	12.5	
	nepheline-syenite	12.5	
	copper carbonate	10	
	iron oxide	10	
Red Lustre #3 (glaze lustre has a very shiny surface and good under heavy reduction)	Gerstley borate	50	
	nepheline-syenite	15	
	borax	50	
	silica	17	
	red copper oxide	10	
	red iron oxide	10	

RAKU REDUCTION METHODS

These are only some of the ways of reducing your work.

Firing Reduction Atmosphere

Reduce the atmosphere in the kiln by reducing the oxygen-to-fuel ratio in the kiln. This can be achieved by simply closing off the flue until you see flames licking up around the flue cavity. This will give you a moderate reduction; some make the flame jump high and, although it looks spectacular, I do not feel that it is necessary. This is called in-kiln reduction; what it does is to increase the amount of carbon from the unburned fuel, which then reacts with the glaze chemicals. Some glazes will give good results with this method, often producing good reds and purples. This procedure must be at least 15 to 20min long for it to take effect.

Post-Firing Reduction Methods

There are many materials that can be used in reduction, they include dry leaves, straw, pine needles, dried seaweed, in addition to the usual sawdust. Frequently these materials will present you with diverse results, so experiment.

Sawdust Reduction
In using a metal bin as a reduction chamber I choose one with a tightly fitting lid, with enough sawdust in the bottom to allow the work to sit comfortably. Fire the kiln to 1000°C or the required temperature of the glaze you are using, then carefully remove the work and immediately place in the bin, pushing the pieces into the sawdust, you then tip enough sawdust over the work to cover it. Place the lid on tightly and securely and leave the work until it is cool enough to be handled. You can then either cool the work down further in water or wait and wash it thoroughly when it is completely cold. Do not do this if the piece is too hot since the shock of the cold water could cause the piece to crack. Note

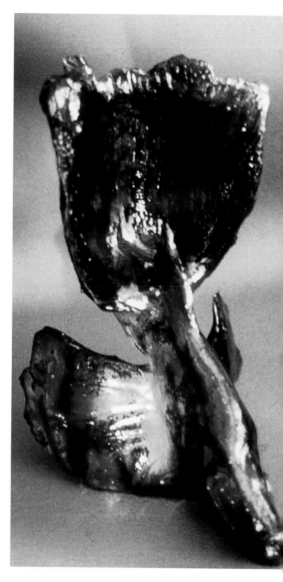

'Gold Fish' (lustre glazes).

that the size of the sawdust fragments, shavings or wood chips can also affect your results, as can the fact that they are either dry or damp. Test before committing your 'special' piece to the bin, it is always better to be safe than sorry.

'Golden Shrine' (back and front). PHOTOS: VICTOR FRANCE

*'Arab' (detail;
Copper Matt).*
PHOTO: VICTOR FRANCE

Copper Matt Effects

There are several methods of obtaining copper matts; this is just one of them: place just enough reducing material, either shredded paper or sawdust, to cover the bottom of a container that will hold the item upright. Fire the piece to approximately 1000°C, remove the glowing work from the kiln and place it immediately into the reduction chamber, letting the flames lick around the piece. Place an airtight lid or cover over the work, making sure that no smoke escapes. You can help stop this smoke escaping by pushing sawdust or wet newspaper against the side of the lid. Leave for about 5 or 10min and then carefully lift the lid up enough to cause the piece to reignite – be careful since the flames may catch you unawares – then quickly reclose the lid and make it airtight. You can do this two or three times during the cooling process and thus see how the colours are progressing. A word of warning: copper matts do fade over time, and, like all copper, it will eventually reoxidize. You can help this by not placing them in direct sunlight. Personally, I like the idea that they are 'living glazes' and watch with interest as they change over the years.

Shredded Newspaper Reduction

This is essentially the same method as with sawdust but using shredded paper instead. I use a first layer of sawdust on the bottom of the reduction bin; this helps to stabilize the pieces. I then put a small amount of shredded paper on top of the sawdust to help with the ignition of the rest of the paper; be careful since this tends to flare up as you place hot work on it. You then tip on more shredded paper. To help to keep in the smoke, you can use wet newspaper or an old, wet towel over the bin before you force the lid on. If I have large pieces or only a few small pieces in one bin, I combine wet paper and a wet towel and then force the lid over the whole. If the lid is too tight to go over both the paper and the towel, put the paper on the bin, then

the lid and place the towel over the closed lid to keep in the smoke.

Sawdust and Wet Newspaper Reduction

Find a flat area, which is not under overhanging trees or anything else that could catch fire. Place a thick enough layer of sawdust on the ground; make sure that you have used enough to hold the work without covering it. Raku fire the work to the correct temperature and then remove each piece from the kiln. Carefully placing the fired work on the sawdust, cover each of the pieces with wet newspaper. Make sure that any smoking areas get more wet newspaper; this helps with the reduction of the work. This is good for small items and works for small areas on the work, but it can be a very smoky process. Always have lots more wet paper available as often the paper burns and needs to be replaced.

Sand Reduction

Place sand to an approximate depth of 200mm in a flat container or take some bricks and make a small enclosed area. You need enough sand to put the work into without its falling over. You will also need to have a container to use as the reduction 'lid' that will fit over the sanded area and give an airtight fit. Lay the fired work in the sand and quickly upend the reduction container over the work and into the sand, pushing sand quickly up against the sides of the container so that no smoke may escape. This technique is not suitable for crackle glazes, since without a source of carbon you get no blacks.

Water Reduction No. 1

Take the work out of the kiln and place it into a large container of water, being careful that the water does not boil over and scald you, or, if the work is a bottle or a container with a small opening, that hot water does not spit out. This is really only useful if you are reducing small items since the thermal shock is often too great for larger items to withstand.

Water Reduction No.2

Half fill a container with water and place some kind of a stand in the centre of it. This must be able to withstand the heat of the work and be able to hold the work above the water. You could use kiln props and shelves as long as they are tall enough. Have a second container that will fit inside the water container and be tall enough to cover the work too. After firing, place the hot work on the stand and quickly cover with the second container. The water makes a barrier and seals air inside. Care must be taken because when the air heats up inside, the water level can rise and touch the work, which may crack through thermal shock.

Pit Reduction

Instead of a container you could dig a pit large enough to take your work. I have used this method when firing very large pieces and did not have a large enough container to use as a reduction bin. The pit prevents the escape of smoke and you have simply to cover the top. This is used in the same manner as a sawdust reduction bin.

I use some fibro board (this is now used as a replacement to asbestos sheeting) to cover the pit and wet newspaper to stop the smoke.

Terra Sigillata

Terra sigillata can be made up with any clay (*see* table, *below*) and it is best to make it with the one you have used for the particular piece you will be putting it on to. Terra sigillata is often used in conjunction with naked raku, as well as normal raku and pit firing. (Calgon is a proprietary water softener.)

Colourants can be added to terra sigillata in the form of stains, for example (quantities in percentages; these can be added to as required): green – 10 per cent to give a medium green, and blue – 10 per cent to give a medium blue. You can also mix the stains together to obtain additional colours.

Raku Slips and Engobes

See table, *right*.

TERRA SIGILLATA			
Glaze Name	**Composition**	**Quantity**	**Description**
Terra Sigillata #1	finely crushed, dry clay	250g	add Calgon to water,
	water	500ml	mix, add clay, and
	Calgon	1g	mix well, leave to settle, discard clear water, use only the centre layer, discard heavy layer with clay
Terra Sigillata #2	ball clay	10.5g	central layer is the
	sodium hydroxide	48g	terra sigillata; add
	water	5ltr	water; can use oxides and stains

RAKU SLIPS AND ENGOBES

Glaze Name	Composition	Weights (g)
Engobe #1	Cornwall stone	40
	frit 4110	15
	kaolin	40
	borax	5
	tin oxide	5
Engobe #2	kaolin	25
	ball clay	25
	silica	20
	frit 4108	30
Bronze Engobe	copper carbonate	30
	manganese dioxide	40
	ball clay	10
	kaolin	20
Raku Slip #1	ball clay	50
	kaolin	25
	talc	10
	frit 4108	15
for red to lustre ADD:	copper carbonate	10%
	red iron oxide	10%
Raku Slip #2	frit 4112	10
	silica	10
	kaolin	10
Raku Slip #3 Kate's	kaolin	30
	silica	10
	frit 4108	60
Copper Resist Slip #1	kaolin	85
	copper oxide	15
glaze to be put over the slip resist	frit 4108	85
	kaolin	15
	fire clay	50
	kaolin	30
	alumina hydrate	20

PORCELAIN SLIP FOR RAKU

See table, *below.*

PATINATION OF COPPER-BASED GLAZES

Heating copper-based glazes with a burner (I use a hand-held blowtorch) produces metallic oxides, which bond themselves to the surface. These can be anything from black to red and brown. The colours will depend on which other materials are present in the glazes. After applying chemicals to these surfaces you can produce colours from black, grey, orange, red, blue and green to dark green. So once again it is wise to test first. You will find that some of the colours and textures will take a day or two to appear and that others change over a couple of weeks, so it is necessary to be patient. You can reheat the work if you wish to work on it still

more or to add to the colour development; it all depends on how well the piece stands up to the heat treatment. I would advise the use of a very good raku clay body or a well-grogged body to prevent any cracking occurring through thermal shock. The usual safety advice applies.

FUMING OF COPPER

Iridescent glaze surfaces may be produced by the use of metallic vapours in a fuming process. Fuming can be carried out in the raku kiln when it is at a dull red heat. By using a metal spoon wired to a long rod you can place the fuming chemicals inside the kiln near the piece, ensuring that the compounds do not touch the work as scumming may occur. Alternatively, you can place the fuming agents on a brick inside the kiln chamber and in the direct path of the flame. By using a chloride spray solution you can treat the hot work immediately after pulling it from the kiln and just before placing it into the reduction

PORCELAIN SLIP FOR RAKU

	Composition	Weights (g)	Description
	kaolin	40	
	ball clay	30	
	potash feldspar	15	
	silica	15	
the following oxides and carbonates can be used to colour the slip:			
	copper oxide	1–4%	blues
	copper carbonate	1–4%	greens
	rutile	3%	cream
	red iron oxide	2%	tan-cream
lustrous surface will also result from reduction when slip containing these compounds is used under a transparent glaze:			
	red iron oxide	10%	
	copper carbonate	10%	

'Ancient Ruin #1' (copper patina).   *'Ancient Ruin #2' (copper patina).*

bin. The chemicals used are in small quantities and include the chlorides of silver, titanium, iron and tin, or any other metallic compound with the ability to vaporize. Note that the vapour is toxic and so I advise you to try this only in an outdoor setting and to make certain that all participants are downwind of the kiln.

PATINATION OF COPPER

Patination can be done either when the work is still hot or after waiting until the piece is cold; after spraying you can heat it up with a blowtorch, gently directing the flame over the sprayed area. You can also spray certain chemicals

95

SUITABLE CHEMICALS

Patination	Chemicals (Toxic)	Amount	Notes
using other chemicals	chloride	5g	spray small amounts;
	liquid soldering flux	100ml	after spraying use a
	stannous chloride	5g	blowtorch or burner;
	ferric chloride	5g	take care not to crack
	copper nitrate	5g	the work
other patination agents are:			
(some of these chemicals can also be used as fuming agents)	tin chloride iron chloride silver chloride titanium chloride vanadium tetrachloride copper sulphate copper nitrate copper chloride potassium polysulphate ferric nitrate ammonium chloride calcium chloride copper sulphate ferrous sulphate		

Salts and Oxides

Colour Washes (try any other oxides and use these measurements as a guide; oxide washes are best to experiment with by volume)	per ½ltr water: ½tsp copper carbonate ½tsp copper oxide ½tsp chrome oxide ½tsp or less cobalt oxide ½tsp or less manganese dioxide		light green–turquoise darker greens–blacks leaf green, opaque dark blue–black brown–purple
Salt washes (crystals are dissolved in water and sprayed on a glazed surface before firing)	bismuth subnitrate copper sulphate stannous chloride barium sulphate iron sulphate		lustre

'Ancient Ruin #3' (copper patina).

on to the work and leave them to dry without heating up. I advise you to test first. The work must, of course, have first been fired with a copper-based glaze for any patination to take effect. Different chemicals will give you different results and textures.

For a blue/green patina, mix 50g of copper nitrate with 100ml of Baker's soldering solution. Heat the area you wish to work on with the burner and then spray on the mixture. Keep up a steady heat until a straw colour starts to appear. Leave to cool over a few days and you will find that a powdery blue/green patina will develop. A range of orange to rust colours may be obtained by using 5g of ferric chloride mixed with 50ml of liquid soldering flux. Place this mixture in a plastic spray bottle and heat the area you wish to treat with a blowtorch or a burner, if it is available. Heat the area so that the liquid can be sprayed onto it without it running down the piece. Keep alternating the heat source with the spray until colour begins to appear. Have a cloth soaked with some of the mixture ready, and place this over the area, leaving it to cool down. To obtain a blue to green colour use 50g of copper nitrate with 100ml of the soldering flux. Test on shards for different results. Keep a good record of which chemicals you used and of what method worked, and take the usual safety precautions.

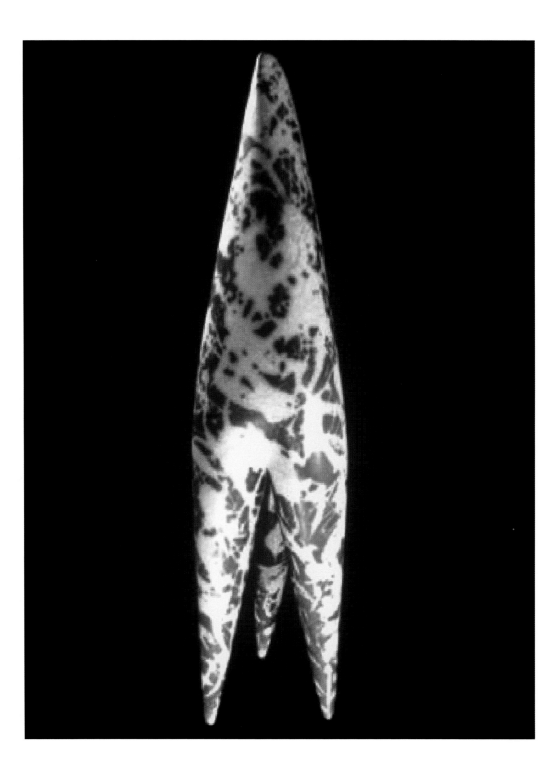

6   INVITED ARTISTS

The people described here are all artists who have been influential in one way or another on my work. They all have a love of what they do and have generously and happily shared their experience with us all, for which I am grateful.

WALLY ASSELBERGHS

CONTACTS: Wally Asselberghs,
Churchilllaan 155 B-2900 Schoten, Belgium
e-mail: wally.asselberghs@scarlet.be
website: www.wallyasselberghs.be
E-Group: nakedraku@yahoogroups.com

Asselberghs received his ceramic training during twelve years of night classes at the Art Academy in Antwerp, completed by several private workshops in Belgium, France and Holland. He has been working in clay for more than twenty-five years, with an original emphasis on stoneware ash glazes and Western raku. After his first initiation in 'naked raku' in 1995, he decided to specialize in this technique and started organizing and teaching workshops in Belgium in 1998. In April 2003 he was invited by Linda and Charles Riggs to teach two weekends of 'combo' workshops in their studio in North Carolina. Participants were trained in the Riggs 'slip-resist' technique, and Wally's 'slip and glaze' method. An article about these sessions appeared in the July 2003 issue of *Clay Times*. A photograph of his work was selected for the recent Lark book *Alternative Kilns and Firing Techniques*, which

OPPOSITE: *'Triamese Woman #2'*
(Wally Asselberghs).

also published his slip-formula in the recipe section. His original focus was on wheel-thrown vases and bowls; more recent works were made by combining coiling techniques and assembling plates, preformed in concave plaster moulds. In his organic objects he tries to find a visual language in which his favourite forms – animals, the human body, rocks and marks left by forces of wind and water – are reduced to their simplest essence and purity. Wally is also the creator and moderator of the International Naked Raku Forum on the Internet, started on a Yahoo Group Web forum three years ago, now joined by more than 500 members from twenty-seven countries, freely sharing and exchanging recipes, photographs, experiences and knowledge about this technique.

The following naked raku technique has been used and refined by Asselberghs. He has kindly allowed me to include his detailed instructions on this unusual and fascinating technique. Yet another variation of raku, it differs only slightly from slip-resist raku. In it a layer of raku glaze is added on top of the slip. The slip acts as a kind of separation layer between the clay and the glaze and prevents the latter from melting on to the surface of the clay piece. The kiln is fired to a temperature of roughly 750–775°C until the glaze starts to bubble. This process must be watched through a peephole in the kiln. Once you have reached this stage, all pieces are removed from the kiln by tongs. When the hot clay is 'reduced' in the smoke-bin, the smoke and carbon will penetrate into the cracks of the glaze, go right through the slip layer into the clay and leave behind an irregular, crack-like pattern on the surface. The layer of slip and glaze will then peel off or will have to be removed with water to reveal the patterns created on the bare or 'nude' clay, hence the name 'naked raku'. Various colour possibilities can be achieved by applying (before polishing) a slip layer containing stains or oxides or by using coloured clay. On those parts where no glaze is applied the clay turns black. After thoroughly cleaning and drying the piece, a thin layer of beeswax is polished into the finished object. This gives a matt, shiny finish, embellishing the surface of the 'naked clay'. Asselberghs discovered naked raku in 1995, during a workshop about primitive firing techniques given by Margot Spiegel Kraemer, who learned the technique herself from Bill and Kate Jacobson.

Naked raku was discovered accidentally in the early 1970s by several people when firing normal raku. There are two methods:

1. *Slip resist:* by Charles and Linda Riggs: very thick clay slurry (alumina, fireclay), 'double dip' variation creates different crackling; an early pioneer was Jerry Kaplan's 'Raku Reduction Stencilling' (flat surfaces). Stencils will only work on a flat surface; a rounded object will not let the stencil lay flat enough to stop the liquid seeping under it.
2. *Slip and glaze:* very thin slip layer with glaze on top; there is a misconception about the reason to apply glaze: not to hold slip on the pot, but to create patterns (Bill and Kate Jacobson, David Roberts (UK)).

The process of naked raku:
■ Smooth surface, two methods:
   terra sigillata: quick method, but can 'pop off' (solution: spraying), also easy to scratch.
   burnishing: gives more 'deep shine' and 'depth of view'.
   — different kind of crackling;
   — favourite burnishing tools: light bulbs, thin plastic (wheel), bone, credit cards, plastic bottom of ice cream boxes, flat stone;

— do not use metal spoons or knives since they leave marks;
— burnishing gives extra strength (good for rims);
— superficial burnishing: matt, rougher surface, less crackling.

After bisque, apply slip layer (separation layer).
■ apply glaze on top of slip;
■ normal raku firing, slightly lower temperature;
■ reduction in smoke bin;
■ remove eggshell: knife, credit card, wood, cleaning pad; use water (scratch risk);
■ remove remnants and let dry completely;
■ apply wax (beeswax, furniture wax), preferably paste type, no liquid wax (deepens the colour: white goes to ivory; protection against dust, grease and finger marks;
■ if there are no good results upon first firing: bisque again to 600–700°C, remove all remnants.

Differences between 'Western raku' and 'naked raku':
■ shiny versus matt : 'subtle shine';
■ primitive aspect of naked raku: final texture is pure result of influences from smoke and fire on the object, no shiny glaze hiding the clay body;
■ idea of sacrificial slip and glaze.

CLAY

Form of the Object
■ Ball-form is the strongest form, preferably made out of a single piece of clay;
■ more risks with constructed forms, flat bowls or plates: outer rim cools faster, shrinks first, causes tensions and results in cracks;
■ equal wall thickness;
■ avoid thin rims and thick bottoms.

Kind of Clay

- Raku clay or commercial clay containing fine grog or sand;
- fine grog: easier to burnish, especially at rims;
- coarse grog can result in white dots or specks in black areas;
- grog is more shock-resistant than sand.

Personal clay recipe (weight or percentage; either will work):
clay recuperation – moistness control – colour possibilities (oxides or stains).
55 clay (any kind)
35 fine grog
10 talc (shock resistant; adds plasticity; grog makes the clay brittle while it is being used).

Colour possibilities before bisque:

- Engobes using oxides or stains;
- risk for pop off due to aggressive nature of firing technique;
- spraying gives stronger bond than brushing;
- suggested to use many thin layers, better than one single, thick application;
- sharp edges and rims: difficult to burnish.

SLIPS

I started experimenting from scratch with pure clay mixtures: earthenware clay, stoneware, porcelain, ball clay, kaolin, powder clay and recuperated clay; most of them work, but some 'plastic' clays curl up, or flake off leading to black areas. David Roberts's technically perfect recipe is: 60g kaolin (EPK) and 40g flint (quartz or silica); the drawback is that it needs constant stirring (heavy silica sinks to the bottom of a slip bucket). My personal slip recipe: is: 50g Limoges (dark grey French stoneware clay), 30g kaolin (EPK), 20g flint (finest quartz or silica) and water: 175g to 100g dry material. The American equivalents for Limoges are: Highwater Phoenix Stoneware clay, Laguna 52 Buff: WC-851; water: 183g to 100g dry material.

The following points are important:

- correct viscosity (looks and feels like full-cream milk); if too thin, the glaze will melt down to the bisqued piece or will be difficult to remove; if too thick, the slip might curl up or flake off, resulting in large black areas;
- the thickness of slip layer also influences the kind of crackling: a very thin slip layer, on smooth burnished surfaces leads to thin, sharp lines, but a thick slip layer on rough surfaces leads to wider lines and hazier crackling;
- sieving (80 or 100 mesh) five or six times when preparing a new slip bucket, removing grog and sand particles to avoid overload of 'black points'; sieve again after using for a couple of hours and stir frequently; avoid air bubbles (no paint mixer immediately before use).

Applying Slip

- Brushing: irregular slip thickness: risk of thin areas; if too thick may create flaking or curling;
- dipping: timing is critical, needs quick action to avoid thick slip layer building up;
- spraying: for complicated forms only, needs good spraying technique: difficult to judge slip thickness, bad mix if silica sinks down in spray container, time consuming;
- pouring: best method: easy, fast, correct thickness, application: hand-held or using sticks, clamps or other tools.

Black points may result from: unsieved grog or sand, dust on surface of bisque or in small cavities (bad burnishing), air bubbles.

GLAZE

Classic recipe (Bill and Kate Jacobson): 35g Gerstley borate, 65g frit 3110, 135g of water to 100g of dry material; as alternatives for Gerstley borate, colemanite and borocalcite are unsuccessful; frit 3221 or 3134 (or low-temperature boron-calcium-potash frit) are acceptable;

standard raku glaze (such as white crackle Raku); new products: Laguna borate.

Alternative recipes are: 75g frit 3110 + 25g nepheline-syenite (low-temperature-firing feldspar); 66g frit 3110 + 33g frit 3221 or 65g frit 3110 + 15g frit 3221 + 20g nepheline-syenite. The viscosity should be 'cream' to 'liquid yoghurt'; when applying sieve before use, stir regularly; glazes with Gerstley borate can be kept for weeks and reused; if for a longer period they may dry out completely, in which case break apart, add water again and sieve. Glaze layer may be applied by spraying with compressor, dipping, brushing or pouring. For other methods *see* later (surface treatment).

Problems between the Slip and the Glaze Layer

In classic glazing: only one or two layers on bisque; in naked raku there is a double layer of slip and a double layer of glaze. The problem is that bisque cannot cope with an overdose of water. The solution is to keep thin rims uncovered or employ only partial glazing, or to dry in between (sun, electric kiln, BBQ, hairdryer or paint burner). Note that the slip layer must be dry (have changed colour) before applying glaze. There should be no problem to glaze-slipped bisque next day, week or month, but avoid dust, and do not apply glaze on areas not covered with slip.

SURFACE TREATMENTS

- Patterns: selective application of glaze on chosen areas;
- masking tape: use best quality (paper-like, not plastic-like), creates sharp clean lines, but can also be torn or cut for irregular patterns;
- latex: only to be used on perfect burnished objects (latex parts left behind in crevices can create burnt plastic marks);
- wax resist: for naked raku (better alternative

for latex), burns away in kiln and can create hazy lines, experiment: slip and glaze over dried-up wax resist, then partly scratched;
- sgraffitto (scratching lines): needs equal slip and glaze layer, scratch with sharp tool down to bisque, best results obtained when glaze has just dried up and is still moist; variation: partly remove glaze between lines with a knife or sponge;
- brushwork;
- spatter with toothbrush;
- dripping down with brush (letting the glaze drip down the brush onto the work);
- squeezing: with injection needle or slip trailer;
- sponging;
- splashing technique: use 'thick glaze' for creating large white areas with big brush, use 'basic glaze' for adding patterns in between, create thin lines by splashing with various sizes of small brush;
- diluted glazes: thin glaze: extra 150ml water (total 285ml water to 100g dry material), use brushwork to paint on slip, intensity of off-whitish to grey areas depends on amount of glaze absorbed by brush and method of application; very thin glaze: extra 225ml water (total 360ml water to 100g dry material), can be poured to create grey areas, drawback: difficult to remove carbonized slip layer, needs long soaking in water.

KILN FIRING

Objects must be absolutely dry before entering the kiln, to avoid explosions. Heat the objects up on a BBQ, in an electric kiln for 20min or on top of a hot kiln. It is important to avoid direct contact between objects and the burner flame – construct some kind of firing chamber.

Firing Cycle

- Slow initial firing so that you can check with a cold bottle for moistness at the exit hole;
- steady firing up to 500°C for 15min;

- quicker firing from 500°C up to 750°C;
- use lower flame from 700 to 725°C;
- start looking into the kiln for 'orange peel' effect (750–775°C);
- short period of maturing (5min): allow orange peel to develop on all sides and objects;
- never exceed 800°C because the glaze will melt;
- consider the cold and hot areas in the kiln and change flame direction if needed.

Reducing after Firing

- Remove with tongs; try to keep the transit time to the smoke bin as short as possible;
- adjust size of smoke bin to size of work;
- reduce with combustible material, sprinkled wood chips work best; keep smoke bin closed for 10–12min, longer for monumental or constructed work;
- allow to cool until 'hand warm', then remove eggshell, clean thoroughly in a water bucket, keep moist when scratching off remnants, give a final clean with clear water; after drying apply a layer of beeswax and buff with a shoe brush, or old cotton tee-shirt or wool rag.

'Cold Air' Variations

Apply in between kiln and smoke bin, this will create wild, dark crackling. Suitable tools: hose from a compressor, air gun, bicycle pump or air spray bottle.

CONCLUSIONS

- Take notes, make drawings;
- remove masking tape and latex before drying on BBQ or in kiln;
- keep bottoms free of glaze;
- do not apply glaze direct to bisque;
- expect the unexpected; await the gifts of the fire gods:
- constantly experiment;
- the final result will be a balance of factors:

kind of clay (porosity), bisque temperature (I use 900–950°C depending on the clay), smoothness of surface (terra sigillata or good–bad burnishing), the form of the object, the temperature of bisque before applying slip (moist studio or hot sun), slip components, slip viscosity, the method of applying slip, thickness of slip layer, the glaze composition, the kiln firing temperature (hot or cold spot), kiln atmosphere, time passing between kiln and smoke bin, the amount and kind of reduction material, the time inside the smoke bin.

STEVEN BRANFMAN

Studio: The Potters Shop, 31 Thorpe Road, Needham Heights, MA 02494, USA

Branfman enjoys an international reputation as a potter, writer, teacher and businessman. He is the founder of The Potters Shop and School, a gallery, school, workshop, bookstore and his studio in Needham, Massachusetts. He travels, presenting guest workshops of his pottery forming, glazing and firing techniques, and has been all over the USA as well as Canada, Mexico, Switzerland, Germany, Belgium and Holland. Steven lives in Newton with his wife Ellen.

Branfman was born in 1953 in Los Angeles and grew up in New York and credits a rich cultural childhood as being the influence that led him to an art career. He was further influenced by a dynamic high school art teacher, particularly in the area of sculpture. He studied art at Cortland State University, New York with Gerald Diguisto (sculpture), George Dugan (drawing) and John Jessiman (pottery). He received his graduate degree at Rhode Island School of Design, working under Norm Schulman and Jun Kaneko. He says of RISD, 'The time spent at RISD was the most influential and important experience in my development as an artist. The teachers were dedicated, the students were

OPPOSITE PAGE:
TOP: *'Bowl' (multi-fired Beherns glaze).*

BOTTOM LEFT: *'Vessel' (multi-layered commercial glaze).*

BOTTOM RIGHT: *'Vessel' (multi-layered stoneware and raku).*

serious, and the atmosphere was exciting and productive.'

Branfman has been an independent studio potter since 1975. In 1977 he founded his studio, The Potters Shop, which has become a nationally known studio, school and artists' workspace, and he now enjoys an international reputation as a potter, teacher and writer. He is the author of two books, *Raku: A Practical Approach* and *The Potters Professional Handbook* published by Krause Publications and the American Ceramic Society, respectively. Steven has delivered numerous workshops and presentations and his work has been exhibited in many one-person and group shows throughout the USA. Steven has been the subject of and has authored many articles on clay. Articles about or by him have appeared in *Ceramics Monthly*, *The Crafts Report*, *Clay Times*, *The Boston Globe*, *Studio Potter* and *Pottery Making Illustrated*, among others. His clayworking techniques, examples of his work, and personal profiles appear in many books on pottery and ceramics as well as *Who's Who in American Art* and *Who's Who Among America's Teachers*.

Steven's concern is to make good pots, pots that hold up to thousands of years of ceramic history. His statement says, 'My work is about vessels and the characteristics that make the vessel come alive: volume, texture, colour and scale. One of my objectives is, through my vessels, to preserve the connection between contemporary ceramic expression and pottery's origins as functional containers, not to transform and abandon it. Though my forms are not functional as in domestic ware, they do suggest function and are certainly containers.' His work appears in private, corporate and museum collections and has been exhibited in galleries and museums throughout the USA.

RAKU GLAZING AND FIRING NOTES

Raku is a technique that is simple in concept, requires rudimentary firing facilities, and is easy to do. Because of this simplicity, many wares display superficial aesthetics and lack individuality and power. A deeper understanding of the process along with experimentation and higher expectations can yield sophisticated colours, textures and surfaces not necessarily recognized as raku. After many years of working with so-called 'raku glazes', that is, glazes designed and formulated to be fired in the Western raku style at the low temperatures of raku (926–1037°C), a glaze labelling accident led me to the use of high-fire glazes. The results were a surprise in that, even though the glaze did not melt enough to fuse completely on to the surface of the ware, there was some melting and, in combination with the raku glazes on the pot, the stoneware glaze offered a subtle, pastel-like effect that was worth further exploration. Today, my work incorporates the use of raku glaze, mid- and high-fire glazes and commercial low-fire glazes in a variety of categories, including special effects glazes and majolica.

When I use stoneware or mid-range glazes I choose them according to the materials contained in them, paying most attention to oxides, other colourants and opacifiers. I use these as one might use a slip. If the stoneware glaze is left uncovered without a low-fired or raku glaze over it, there will be no colour and any post-firing smoking will turn the surface grey to black, just as it does to the raw clay. Because I am using glazes that run the gamut of maturity, from the lowest melting temperature to the highest, with each offering different effects depending on the firing temperature, I never use cones or a pyrometer. Instead, I rely on my observation of the surfaces and remove the ware when I see the surface that I am after. Glazes may be very dry, just flowing and lava-like, satin, glossy or any combination. Visual observation and decision making require practice and experience, but ultimately it is the most effective way to control your results. It is important to understand that all of my firing remains in the low-fire range.

I apply my glazes by the traditional methods of pouring, dipping, spraying and brushing, though most application is by brushing multiple, thin layers, alternating between glazes. Over the years I have collected about 500 jars of unwanted and discarded commercial glazes. I arrange them on my shelf by name, colour and description and I never test before using them, I make what often appears to be a random selection of perhaps ten or so and arrange them on my table by colour and description, looking not so much to predict the colours (though I have gotten pretty good at it) but rather to juxtaposition my expectations of contrast, opacity, tone and texture. I may apply as many as twenty or more layers, using inexpensive, Chinese, stiff, bristle brushes available at the hardware store.

It is important to understand the concept of fluxing action when combining glazes of different maturing temperatures. The flux, or melting component in a low-temperature glaze, will cause a high-temperature glaze to melt at a lower temperature. This is helpful in predicting and controlling surface and glaze texture.

My kiln of choice is a top-loading, converted electric kiln and I fire with high-pressure (7–10lb/sq in) propane. Being very conservative in my firing cycle, I always fire from a cold kiln and never preheat my pots to do successive firings in the same kiln. With six kilns there is no need to do that. My cycle is from 2 to 4hr, depending on the size of the pieces. Longer firing times have all but eliminated breakage, but, more importantly, they encourage richer, deeper and more sophisticated surfaces. I will often soak glazes at different times during the cycle and at the end of the firing. I also often fire in an electric kiln, not a converted electric kiln. I choose this when I am looking for the brightest, cleanest glaze results on my ware. Even when firing in an oxidation atmosphere, whenever you are using a fuel-fired kiln there is going to be some small amount of reduction. In an electric kiln you will get an atmosphere that is clear of any reduction. I simply load the work and turn the kiln on high. In about 2–3hr the kiln has reached the temperature slowly and evenly and the work is ready to be removed and reduced in the normal manner. I also vary the firing atmospheres when firing in fuel kilns. Most of the time I fire in an oxidizing atmosphere, but occasionally I put the pots through a period of reduction to alter the glaze effects. Reduction can have a variety of effects, including copper reds, deep blues and other unusual colours and depth. Reduction must be moderate to heavy and be carried out for at least 30 to 40min. Moderate to heavy is evident by cutting back on the primary air or closing the flue just enough to see flame and smoke coming from the kiln.

Post-firing technique includes a short period (30sec to 1min) of cooling the ware, usually by spraying the glazed surface with water. The cooling encourages colour development and reduces or eliminates copper and metallic lustre. Spraying also allows for selective cooling by adjusting the spray width and spraying only where I want to. I avoid spraying unglazed surfaces so as to not discourage carbonization and the resulting black surface. I reduce in metal containers with coarse sawdust, wood shavings or dry pine needles. Once the ware is in the container I leave it to cool to the touch. All of my work is then

'Vessel' (white slip/New Roger's Black (Jared's variation)).

'Vessel' (Del Favero lustre).

scrubbed aggressively with an abrasive cleanser to remove ash, soot and other residues.

PERSONAL STATEMENT

Art has always been a part of my life. My mother was a graduate of the Julliard School, studying piano, bassoon and she spent some time drawing. Her grandfather, a Russian immigrant who lived with us when I was a child, was a tailor of fine clothing. My great uncle, also from Russia and to whom I was very close, painted landscapes while he made his living as a house painter. My uncle was a talented painter and musician. My parents saw the value in art and

took my siblings and me to museums, concerts, Broadway plays and, to our chagrin, forced us to take music lessons. Despite all this, I was more interested in athletics than arts and went to college to become a physical education teacher. That career path didn't last very long. There was never a conscious decision to do art or to become an artist. It's not the kind of activity one decides to do. It's more like something that gets done because it has to.

My movement towards art was natural and I knew it was right. Clay entered my life as a random encounter in 1971. John Jessiman, my teacher, was an Alfred grad who was a wonderful potter and teacher. He mesmerized me with his fluidity and ease with clay. After seeing him throw I decided I wanted to be a potter. At Rhode Island School of Design, Norm Schulman was unforgiving, rigid and set in his ways. I learned a lot from Norm and the whole scene there. I've been involved with clay full time since 1975 making pots, teaching, writing and operating my own studio. From my earliest introduction to clay I have always been fascinated and excited about the wheel. It is not one, but all of the components of that tool that hold and keep my interest: the speed, fluidity and, in particular, the sense of growth I observe and control during the process. My aim and ambition is to make good pots.

Raku technique and process have held my attention for over thirty years, and throughout this time the primary attraction for me has remained the never-ending variations of applied technique, the spontaneity of the actual firing process and the always present degree of surprise and serendipity in the results. Raku is a practice that offers the best of all worlds for me. The method is deeply rooted in tradition and I approach it with the utmost respect for the technique and its origins. And, while its origins serve as a constant reminder to me of where the craft has evolved from, its contemporary incarnation is very different. So I can work simultaneously in a traditional method where all the rules have been established and a contemporary technique where the rules are constantly in question.

Raku firing is fast by its design and spontaneous by my nature. When the piece is ready to be taken from the kiln there is a lot of chaotic looking activity for a very short time. It does, however, require exacting cooperation between myself, my equipment, my assistants and the fire. Though there is always a degree of surprise, the success of the work depends on my ability to command and predict the variables of material and fire. It is like a dance that, when choreographed well, flows into a statement of beauty. It feels good when done right!

I enjoy the challenge of working large, not just to achieve size but to arrive at the right size for a particular piece. My largest pieces are done using a variation on the Korean coil and throw technique. Thick coils are carefully attached to the rim of a leather-hard form and pulled up to continue that form. There is almost no size limitation, thus I must always be in touch with my design and intentions. The actual raku firing of large work presents its own challenges and it is the search for answers to some of these questions that often results in new creative directions and discoveries for me.

My vessel forms have matured in concert with my personal aesthetic vision. Integral to the development of successful and satisfying shapes is the importance of their surfaces and how those surfaces contribute to the understanding, interpretation and significance of the finished ware. To this end, my pots often have distorted surfaces that are highly textured or carved. The incorporation of dry clay applications, grog, sand and glass into the surfaces are also techniques that have contributed to the aesthetic growth of my wares. Efforts to achieve mastery of a palette of glazes are a challenge that in and of itself leads to discoveries of colour, texture, surface and form. By its very nature, art work is a reflection or portrait of one's self. Work that is honest must come from within the artist and is the most valid. My most successful work is that which I feel closest to during its growth. Whether you want to admit it or not, all art is portraiture and some pieces make you look better than others.

My work has always been about form and my vessels have matured in concert with my personal aesthetic vision. Integral to the development of successful and satisfying shapes is the importance of their surfaces and how those surfaces contribute to the understanding, interpretation and effectiveness of the finished ware. Shapes grow from the bottom up and the inside out. Volume, pressure, breath and interior presence must be expressed and communicated.

My forming method of expanding the ware from the inside out without touching the surfaces alters, personalizes and gives life to these applications. A technique that holds a lot of interest for me is the use of inlaid and pressed glass as both an element of colour and texture. The use of glass has proved to be both an aesthetic and a technical challenge.

Efforts to achieve mastery of a palette of glazes is a challenge that in and of itself leads to discoveries of colour, texture, surface, and form. Though my ware is fired in the cone 010–07 range, I use glazes of different maturing temperatures, including so called raku glazes, standard low-fire recipes, mid-range and high-fire stoneware and porcelain formulations as well as commercial glazes varying in temperature and style, underglazes, overglazes, slips, engobes and oxide washes. Also contributing to colour and texture are slips and dry clay and glaze mixtures that are often applied to the wet clay surfaces during the forming process instead of the usual application on bisque ware. Glazes are brushed, poured and sprayed in multiple layers of varying thicknesses. I fire in electric and fuel-fired kilns with oxidation and reduction atmospheres. Low-fire salt and soda firing and fuming have also become more important to my work.

Post-firing technique is important yet is often overlooked as a creative influence on the finished wares, and this too is an area that occupies much of my creative energies. It is frequently treated as a rigid procedure that must be followed according to certain instructions that are not variable. It is, in fact, greatly variable and the method of post-firing treatment will greatly influence the wares. I will vary the type of combustible material, the amount of material to use and the length of time the ware is exposed to the material. Compressed air, water and fuming sprays are all part of the post-firing phase.

Branfman's Glazes

Most of the commercial low-fire glazes in my collection are Amaco glazes. This is only by chance, not choice. I have used glazes by many different manufacturers in the USA as well as throughout Europe with equally good results. Though commercial low-fire glazes will often yield similar colours in raku as in standard low fire, the same cannot be said for mid- and high-fire glazes. Choosing glazes that will be successful requires experimentation and a sense of how materials react to firing.

Recipes are in percentages by weight.

Behern's Raku Cone 016	
frit p 25	
(substituted ferro #3269)	
frit 3134	
lithium carbonate	9.9
EPK (Edgar Plastic Kaolin)	6.2
(any quality of kaolin can	
be substituted)	
flint 325m	14.0

ADDITIONS:
vanadium stain (experiment with different strengths and varieties)
copper carbonate
cobalt carbonate

Basic White Crackle	
Gerstley borate	65
Tennessee ball clay	5
nepheline-syenite	15
flint	5
tin oxide	12
My favourite and most reliable white crackle	

New Roger's Black (Jared's Variation)	
Custer (American Potash Feldspar)	20
Gerstley borate	80
red iron oxide	12
cobalt carbonate	5
black copper oxide	5

Deep, dark blue to black; areas that are heavily reduced will result in copper lustre

Del Favero Lustre	
Gerstley borate	80
Cornwall stone	20
copper carbonate	2

Reduce only moderately for a fine turquoise crackle; if heavily reduced a copper lustre will result

Kelley's Low-fired Shino, Cone 04–08	
lithium carbonate	29
nepheline-syenite	70
EPK	11
light rutile	6
manganese carbonate	5

Semi-opaque glaze with excellent crackle and lovely tan to silvery colour; its characteristics and texture depend on careful observation during firing; once melting has begun, there is only a short period to control the flow of glaze and thus the resulting surface; with care, a very shino-like effect can be achieved; one of my favourite glazes

'Bowl' (Kelly's Low-Fired Shino).

Roger's White	
spodumene	35
Gerstley borate	60
Tennessee ball clay	5
(any ball clay will do)	

This glaze, as are many that are called white, is clear glaze and only white over white clay or slip; the clue is that there is no opacifier (tin oxide, Opax, titanium, Superpax, etc.) in the glaze; every potter's glaze palette should have a clear glaze, I use it to flux high-fire glazes as well as a kind of top coat allowing other colours and textures to show through

Erica's Aqua	
Gerstley borate	80
Cornwall stone	20
tin oxide	5
cobalt carbonate	2
copper carbonate	3

Lovely, medium blue-green with copper flashes in light to medium post-firing reduction; too much reduction will result in copper lustre

Here are two glazes that are wonderful in reduction:

Piepenburg Red Bronze	
frit 3134	50
Gerstley borate	50
tin oxide	3
black copper oxide	2.5

Deep bronze sometimes with tan specs to blood red when heavily reduced; light post-firing reduction

Piepenburg Oil Lustre	
frit 3134	50
Gerstley borate	50
black copper oxide	2.5
manganese dioxide	1

Has effect of an oil spot glaze; reduce in kiln and then light post-firing reduction

GARY FERGUSON

Gary is the publisher of several books on raku and also of an E-magazine. He has been featured in *500 Bowls* (Lark Books, 2003) and *Pottery Making Illustrated* (October 2003). He is the winner of numerous awards for his work, and

Gary Ferguson: 'got raku?'

111

'Raku Cup' (Hawaiian Copper Blue).

continues to attend seminars and workshops to further his knowledge of his craft.

PERSONAL STATEMENT

'So, did you go to school to learn how to do this?', she asked, opening the lid on one of my pieces. 'Unfortunately, I didn't. I studied physics and computer science in college', I reply, watching for the strange look that I know will appear on her face in just a second; of course, I realize how odd it is for a 'computer guy' to be interested in art, but that is my case.

I spend a lot of my time working with computers, which are predictable, controllable and impersonal. This definitely hits one part of my brain. But I do like to spend as much time as I can with clay, which is sometimes unpredictable, very flexible and can evoke emotion or have personality. And, of course, hits a totally different part of my brain. These two mediums seem to provide a balance to my life and are a wonderful way to experience both my logical and my creative side. This theme of extreme opposites is prevalent in many areas of my raku work.

For example, I enjoy the contrast of a clear crackle combined with a copper matt, or a blue matt combined with a glossy blue/copper. I find this much more interesting than all matt, all glossy or all crackle on a piece. An added benefit is that there is often an interesting effect that occurs at the intersection of the two types of glaze that becomes the best part of the piece. I also play with the combination of glazed and unglazed sections on a piece. I will often use wax resist or tape resists, creating precise patterns or pictures on the piece that is then covered with a bright, dynamic glaze. The flashing colours of the glaze are a strong contrast to the exacting dark, black pattern produced from the resist.

Most of my pieces start out wheel-thrown. I like the smooth, symmetrical curves of a wheel-thrown piece, but I like to contrast this with hand-built additions of handles, knobs or special textures, carving or piercing to add more interest to the piece.

I like making all types of pieces: pots, bowls, plates, wall pieces and even jewellery, constantly trying new forms and techniques. But there are a couple of forms that I have made over the years that I really like and continue to create regularly. These are Rocks and Shards.

The rocks I create are not lumps of clay shaped to resemble a rock, but a carved, lidded piece that is approximately the size of a baseball or

'Small Pot' (Rick's Turquoise).

LEFT: *'Rock'*
(bronze/copper).

BELOW:
'Wall Piece' (clear
and turquoise).

softball. This type of piece has evolved greatly from the first version I ever created, which was basically a simple globe shape with a cut lid. They now have thinner walls, intricately carved lids and knobs. And because they are raku-fired, there are certain special methods to creating rocks. The way I create a rock today is to start with about 1 to 1.5lb of clay. I throw a basic cylinder as dry as I can, keeping the inside bottom sponged dry. I then carefully collar in the rim to close the opening completely. When I do this I make sure that there is clay above the closure to create a knob. Since the piece is now closed, with air trapped inside, I use a wooden or metal rib to modify the shape and curve of the piece from the outside. I use an angled, pointed stick to trim excess clay from around the base of the piece when I've finished throwing. This way I don't have to try and trim the piece upside down later. I wire-cut the piece from the bat and allow it to dry a bit before I poke a small hole somewhere in the top, using a pin tool. This will allow the air to escape from the drying piece.

When the piece reaches a somewhat wet, leather-hard stage, I cut various patterns in what will become the lid using a sharp knife. I then create a jagged cut all the way around the piece to create a lid, making sure there are no undercuts that will not allow the lid to be removed. Using this method, the lid will fit on the piece only one way, and will usually stay in place. I then place the piece (with the lid in place) on a kiln stilt to dry very slowly. This needs to dry slowly; otherwise spiral cracks will appear on the inside of the lid.

When the piece is completely dry, it is bisque fired. I place a strip of narrow tape across the gap between the lid and the base to keep the glaze from getting into the crack and sealing the lid in place. I raku-fire them and typically will remove the piece from the kiln in two sections, the lid first and then the base. The melted glaze typically makes the work too slick to remove as one piece from the kiln with tongs.

These pieces look great with a contrast of a copper matt glaze on the base and a clear crackle on the lid.

My second favourite piece is the Shard, or what I call wall art. I started making these pieces using pieces of slabs (shards) that I stuck together using wads of clay to create interesting patterns that could be hung on the wall. The problem was that the survival rate was very low due to the thinness of the joints between the shards. It wasn't worth my time or materials to make them. But I loved the idea and worked out the following method, which gives the same look, but the survival rate is much higher.

First, I wedge a 5lb ball of clay really well. I then create a slab using a rolling pin and quarter-inch board slats. Finally, I let this slab set up a little bit between several sheets of newspaper. When the slab will resist denting with fingers, I place it on a piece of canvas and carve out the overall shape using a wooden trimming tool or a fettling knife. I often trace around a large plastic bat, which is about the largest circumference that I can fire in my kiln. I lightly 'draw' a shard pattern on the slab using a wooden trimming tool. I then cut out sections of the slab with a fettling knife that would not exist if actual shards had been used. Now the joints are not really joints but a continuation of the clay slab, so the survival is much higher.

I place the cut slab upside down on a large, round, domed serving pan (sprayed with WD40) to dry. This gives the piece a concave shape that will help to keep it from warping too much during firing. This, again, has to be dried very slowly to keep from cracking or warping. I bisque fire the shards flat on a bed of sand on a kiln shelf. This seems to make a 'slick' surface for the piece to expand and shrink without cracking. Then it is glazed, leaving most of the drawn connector pieces unglazed. I often glaze the shard pieces with different glazes or create a glaze pattern on one shard and solid glaze on another. This again adds contrast and interest

115

to the piece. I then fire them on edge in my raku kiln to allow easy removal for reduction. I do not place any knobs on the back for hangers, etc., as I prefer to hang these pieces by using nails that can stick through some of the cut-out sections. No chance for the piece to fall off the wall that way.

Every potter has a 'bag of tricks' he or she develops and uses in creating their work. This is often more prevalent in the case of raku artists since they are working with such extreme firing conditions. In my case, I have tape resists, a blowtorch and an unusual reduction process in my bag of tricks.

One technique I use quite a bit is to employ tape as a glaze resist. I use ½in to 1in-wide masking tape to protect the bases of pieces or the rims for lids, instead of wax resist. It is much less messy. I also use very narrow tape, ⅛in to ⅙in wide, to create a variety of patterns on a piece that will turn black during the post-firing reduction. I often use this method to create Celtic knot patterns or Chinese lattice patterns on a piece. The narrow tape can also be used as a divider between two glazes that I do not want to mix during firing. For example, I will use narrow tape to create a pattern around the top of a piece, and then glaze the bottom with copper matte and the rim with clear crackle. The narrow tape will help to keep the copper glaze and the clear glaze separated during application via a brush. You can use pin striping or lettering tape found in office supply stores for these types of application, but I find it is fairly expensive. A much cheaper option is to use quilter's tape (usually available in both ¼ and ⅛in widths) found in craft stores. If all else fails, buy ½in masking tape and slice it in half.

I sometimes use a small hand blowtorch for two different processes in creating a piece, once during throwing and again after post-firing reduction. I use the blowtorch during throwing

THIS PAGE:
'Carved Rim Pot'
(clear and crackle and shinju).

OPPOSITE PAGE:
'Celtic Knot Urn'
(tape resist, Gary's Green and Clear Crackle).

when I'm trying to throw a piece with severe curves and I don't want to wait for the piece to dry, or if a piece got too wet during the throwing process and is threatening to collapse. This works best if the piece is allowed to spin slowly on the wheel as I move the blowtorch up and down over the areas I want to dry. I do this both from the inside and the outside. This will typically firm up the piece enough to finish forming without collapsing.

Most people know that if you do not like the results of a firing, you can typically refire the piece and get different results, but sometimes if I get too much copper (in my opinion), I will use the blowtorch to change the results. You have to be very careful in using this technique because, if you heat one section of a piece too much, it can crack, pop or explode. It is a good

idea to wear safety goggles when doing this. If you remove the piece from your reduction chamber and the piece is totally copper and you were hoping for some blues or greens, try placing the piece on a brick or metal can and then passing the flame of a blowtorch over different sections of the piece to heat the glaze more. As the glaze is heated, it will begin to reoxidize and you will start to see flashes of colours round the areas that are being heated. Do not do this too much or you will lose all your copper colour. When you have finished, dunk the piece in water to freeze the glaze. I have seen this technique used to the extreme to form many circles of colour, which created a peacock feather effect.

Probably the most unusual reduction method that I use is when firing the glaze called Rick's turquoise (*see* recipe below). If I reduce this glaze

in a 'normal' reduction method, such as in a closed can with combustibles, I get a coppery bronze with some green flashing. It's pretty, but not as dynamic as it could be. The special reduction method I use involves a metal tub that I line with wads of newspaper, in essence making a nest of newspapers in the tub. I fire the piece to maturity, remove it from the kiln with tongs and hold it in the air for about 5sec. Next, I place the piece in the nest of paper and let it start to burn for about 20 to 30sec. Finally, I grab a water hose and use a nozzle with a fine mist setting and begin to spray the piece with a fine mist. This creates a huge amount of steam and extinguishes the flame. I continue to spray the piece until it is cool enough to pick up with gloved hands and then put it in a bucket of water to finish cooling. By using this method I

get yellow, blue, green, red, turquoise and copper all on the same piece. It is the most unusual raku glaze I use. I am constantly trying new glazes, but I do have a few that I use pretty regularly. The following are all mixed by weight.

Hawaiian Copper Blue	
Gerstley borate	80
bone ash	20
copper carbonate	5
cobalt oxide	2.5
tin oxide	1.3

There are several variations of this, one being Hawaiian blue, which has the same recipe but with all the colourant quantities doubled. This is a nice, blue, matt glaze that can flash copper, green and burgundy. It will become a semi-gloss glaze if it is fired at too high a temperature (over 1700°F (927°C)). It seems to work better when applied fairly thinly. I usually reduce this in a can lined with sheets of newspaper, with a handful of shredded paper thrown on top before closing the container.

Gary's Green Crackle	
Gerstley borate	65
nepheline-syenite	20
EPK	5
silica	10
copper carbonate	3

THIS PAGE:
'Moon Vase' (clear crackle/turquoise).

OPPOSITE PAGE:
'Abstract Plate' (various glazes).

Yes, this is a glaze I created, or at least derived from a clear crackle glaze. It typically produces a glossy medium to dark green crackle glaze, with some copper flashing if heavily reduced. It works better if applied heavily.

Rick's Turquoise	
Gerstley borate	33
nepheline-syenite	17
spodumene	17
lithium carbonate	17
Zircopax	16
copper carbonate	2.2

This is the glaze I referred to above that I use in the special post-fire reduction technique. The glaze has to be fired a little hotter than most raku glazes (cone 04 to cone 02) to mature properly.

3110 Clear	
frit 3110	100
tin oxide	3
bentonite	3

This is about as simple a glaze as you can get, it is a white, glossy glaze that can have an orange-peel texture along with crackle and some pin

holing possible. It should be applied fairly thickly. You can also add copper carbonate (3) and get a wonderful turquoise with the same texture and some copper flashing if heavily reduced.

I mentioned that I constantly experiment with raku glazes and have compiled a collection of glazes in my first book *Raku Glazes: The Ultimate Collection; Over 360 Recipes and More* (2nd edn). I also provide a sampling of free raku glaze recipes on my website at www.garyrferguson.com. I am constantly learning and experimenting with raku techniques and I have compiled what I have learned so far in my second book *Raku Secrets: The Complete Guide of Amazing Raku Results*. Since 2003 I have been publishing a free monthly newsletter called *Just Raku* (www.justraku.com), which covers the whole range of raku and is read by raku artists all over the world.

I have been involved in raku since 1995 when my hands first touched clay on a wheel and I could smell the raku smoke of a post-firing reduction. I guess the reason I love the clay medium so much is the almost unlimited options that are available to the artist, and the rapid and dynamic raku process continues to excite and challenge me. It is great having a medium that allows for constant experimentation with unlimited possibilities.

I live in Idaho with my wife Gina, our two very busy boys Connor and Trevor, and an ever changing assortment of cats and dogs. I can be contacted at: pottery@garyrferguson.com.

DAVID JONES

Born in 1953 in the United Kingdom, David graduated in philosophy and literature from Warwick University and it was during this period that he discovered ceramics. He has studied

'Dark Towers'. PHOTO: ROD DORLING

'Deep Bowl' (silver lustre). PHOTO: ROD DORLING

and worked in Japan as a recipient of the INAX Design Prize for European Ceramics and is a fellow of the Craft Potters of Great Britain. In 1999 he published his book *Raku: Investigations into Fire* (The Crowood Press). Currently he is senior lecturer in ceramics at the University of Wolverhampton www.davidjonesceramics.co.uk.

Raku is a remarkable technique because we can manipulate the entire spectrum of effects from just a limited range of chemicals, simply mixed into glazes, just by the careful observation of the fire within the kiln itself. The potter, by grabbing a pot from the fire just as it begins to melt, will produce a tight, crystalline surface; when the flame is reflected from the glaze surface then the clay is unctuously engulfed in soft, runny, treacly glaze. Glaze in raku works in the same way that clothing is used to enhance the human body. Sometimes it functions like a gaudy outfit to draw attention to the wearer; at another time it can be the formal presentation to the public represented by a sober suit. Within raku all permutations are possible. The skin can be left naked, or perhaps highlighted by the nuance of a fine spray of terra sigillata. The cloth can be caressingly thin or obscuringly thick, flowing and pooling densely in every crevice. We can suggest flowing movement by directing the glaze to slide over the contours of our work by firing higher than normal. A cooler firing, utilizing the same glazes, will communicate a stiffness or an awkwardness as the dry surface of the not-quite-flowing glaze fails to quite fit the undulations of the clay.

Raku requires careful orchestration to achieve these qualities; the subsequent removal, red-hot

– or cooler – from the kiln and the moving of it to a bin of combustibles will allow new glints of secondary reduction to play across the surface and to plunge the skin, covered in terra sigillata, to a deep black. We know from long experience the different qualities and effects from secondary reduction; these cannot be precisely foretold. It is the orchestration of the effects, a combination of timing, removal and the qualities of reduction materials and length of time spent in smoking which allow an almost limitless palette to be used for expression.

Glaze	
alkaline frit	85g
china clay	10g
bentonite	5g
silver nitrate	1.5g

Terra Sigillata
2ltr distilled or rain water
1kg fine powdered clay
1tsp sodium silicate

Mix these materials together, leave overnight, siphon off the water and collect the next layer of terra sigillata; dispose of heavy settled clay; paint or spray on until a soft sheen appears; burnishing with cling film wrapped around the finger can produce extra shine.

'Untitled' *(detail).* PHOTO: ROD DORLING

MIKE KUSNIK

Mike was born in the former Czechoslovakia in 1927, and graduated as a ceramic chemist in 1947. Arriving in Australia in 1950, he, like so many migrants, held down many different jobs, until around 1953 when he was approached by two Czechs who invited him to join them in establishing a ceramic studio. Mike went to Western Australia in 1959 as a research and development chemist for a local company. In 1969 Ray Samson, the then head of the Art Department of Perth Technical Collage, asked Mike to take a few pottery classes. This led to a full-time teaching position at the Western Australian Institute of Technology, now Curtin University. Mike is well known to all ceramicists as someone who is generous in giving advice and expertise, and the Western Australian ceramic community has been especially lucky in being able to have the benefit of his knowledge and his untiring help. In 1997, in recognition of his services to ceramics, Mike was presented with the Medal of the Order of Australia, a well deserved reward.

Raku originated in Japan from a fast production of glazed roofing tiles. The speed of the glazing and firing was readily accepted by the traditional pottery craftsmen to produce vessels for tea ceremonies. In our part of the world, it is one of the most enjoyable branches of ceramics. It has many attributes, for example, cheap materials as well as low firing costs to reach and wow any beginners as well as professionals. The most attractive aspect of raku is the almost instant access to view the finished product.

Any clay body may be used for raku as long as it is biscuit-fired to the appropriate temperature-maturity as recommended by the clay manufacturer. One has to take into consideration that an under-fired body, unglazed or glazed, may suffer from moisture expansion and fretting, especially if the art object is made for open display, for instance, in a garden. All creations made for inside display (sheltered from rain) can be made and fired as you please.

The best raku clay mix would be good plastic clay (50 per cent) with an addition of grog to about 35 per cent (fired china clay) of two or three particle sizes (30, 40 and 60 mesh) and 15 per cent of whiting. Fire to maturity at 1060–1100°C. This mix would give you low wet to dry shrinkage and also low dry to fired shrinkage. The coefficient of thermal expansion of the fired body would also be low – good for heat shock but not so good for a glaze fit. You may ask, who cares about the glaze fit? As far as we know, most raku pots are made for decoration only and with all types of surface treatment, ranging from colourful high gloss to matt-dry surface achieved by fuming and other chemical treatments. But in the opinion of the writer, faux glazes are the best and fastest solution in decorating raku. In other words, the whole job can be done in a simple glazing and firing operation as long as you know your glazes. Biscuit pots are glazed with appropriate glazes, fired and reduced in sawdust (the red-hot pots have to hit the sawdust while the glaze is still pyroplastic) to develop copper reds and very colourful lustres, including gold. Alternatively, the glazed pots can be fired to maturity and than reduced (relight the burners and turn off the primary air) in the kiln during the cooling time at 700–800°. Naturally, the pots will lack the black, unglazed surface; but do not despair – this can be achieved with subsequent black firing in a small rubbish bin on a bed of pine needles and cones in a very short time.

Some of the best raku glazes are made from commercially produced frits (all figures are weight percentages).

Component	Glaze A	Glaze B	Glaze C
frits (equal weights ferro 4108, 4110)	100	100	100
tin oxide	4	4	4
manganese dioxide	8	–	–
ferric oxide	–	8	–
copper oxide	–	–	3
bentonite	3	3	3

All test glazes should be fired to about 1000°C ± a few degrees, depending on the fineness of your materials and the firing schedule. Notice that the base glaze contains little alumina, thus making it possible to use large additions of metallic oxides without saturating the glaze. This is an advantage, favouring lustre development under reduction. Add water to each glaze with care; you may need approximately 650ml for 1kg of dry glaze. Make sure each mix has the same amount of water because the blending is based on volumetric measures, that is, a spoon or an eggcup. There may be very slight discrepancies due to the smaller amount of copper, nevertheless, it will give you a very good idea which way to turn.

And now blend the three glazes together on a triaxial principal: each step represents one part. You finish up with three base glazes and twelve blended glazes.

```
            A
          1   2
        3   4   5
      6   7   8   9
    C  10  11  12  B
```

Just to give you a start: Glaze No.4 contains 2 parts A, 1 part B and 1 part C; Glaze No.7 contains 1 part A, 1 part B and 2 parts C; and Glaze No.11 contains 2 parts B and 2 parts C. Thoroughly mix all the ingredients and apply them on test pieces to be fired side by side in your test kiln or with your other firings. The test firing can be carried out under oxidizing condition; the results will give you good indications of which samples to try under raku firing. If you have a small gas test kiln, fire the samples under reduction when cooling (800–700°C). Make sure to mark each test correctly as you may doubt some of the results.

And now you can explore additions of alumina to the base glazes. Add to each base glaze 5, 10 and 15 per cent of hydrated alumina, thus creating three more sets of triaxial diagrams of a further thirty-six glazes. Your mind will boggle when you see the results. And, of course, you can also use chromium, cobalt and nickel with the oxides of iron, manganese and copper, together with titanium dioxide to bring in more variations.

The potters who do not like glazing and prefer naked raku could improve their success with paperclay to wrap around the biscuit pot. The paperclay should have a low wet-to-dry shrinkage and slightly increased dry-to-fired shrinkage. The best paperclay for this job should be an earthenware body, based on 50 per cent clay, 35 per cent silica and 15 per cent whiting with an addition of soft zinc oxide of the order of 5 to 10 per cent, to increase the fired shrinkage and thus cause the paperclay to tear and fall from the pot.

I hope that these few lines will encourage you to develop something new and, please, do not blame me for failures!

ROBYN LEES

Robyn Lees studied visual arts at Edith Cowan University, in Western Australia. She is a teacher and lecturer and has presented workshops on her techniques and methods and currently works full time as an arts practitioner from her studio and gallery in Denmark, situated in the south-west of Western Australia. Robyn has a well-deserved reputation for her highly decorative and, most often, brightly coloured, figurative pieces, sculptures that are based on the female figure. She utilizes these forms to exhibit her expertise with form and decoration. Created into unique, audacious sculptures, jugs and teapots, these figures are quite often whimsical and are made with an ironic sense of humour. She has won many awards and her work is to be found in major collections throughout Australia. Her work is represented in collections at: Queensland University of Technology Art Collection, Joondalup Development Corporation Art Collection, Edith Cowan University Art Collection, Manly Art Gallery and Museum Collection and in several Australian and foreign private collections.

127

'Attachment/Detachment'
(three figures, raku fired).

PERSONAL STATEMENT

I have been working full time as a clay artist since graduating with a Bachelor of Arts, Visual Arts, from Edith Cowan University in 1990. Through the conceptual underpinning of my work, I explore 'the female stereotype' in its various guises. I am concerned that this stereotype, like all stereotypes, simplifies and trivializes complex identity traits. It is a device on which to hang superficial and prejudicial concepts. Despite the influence of the women's movement, the colonial view of women as either 'damn' whores or

'God's police' still informs the contemporary Australian view of women. I express my concerns through the use of 'The Painted Lady', brightly painted, audacious women sculptures referencing utilitarian teapots, jugs, and bowls. They provide a metaphorical reference to the duality demanded of women by society – they should be useful as well as beautiful. My ladies contemplate the women's function and attempt to reference her emotional strength, spiritual aspirations and personal vulnerability. Most of my work begins life on the wheel as voluptuous, symmetrical forms. In a complex distortion and assemblage process, these forms take on life as contorted, farcically idolatrous, female figures.

JEFF MINCHAM

Jeff is well known in Australia and overseas for his large raku-fired pieces, often with an oriental perspective. Since completing his studies at the South Australian and Tasmanian Schools of Art in the early 1970s, he has held seventy solo exhibitions in Australia and exhibited widely overseas. He has taught and lectured throughout Australia and internationally, introducing many established and emerging ceramicists to the art of raku. During his long and distinguished career, Jeff's work has been widely acclaimed for its evocative power, innovation and technical mastery. He works small, and produces exquisite raku-fired teabowls, often with a palm wood box made to go with the teabowls. His new work has undergone a transformation.

PERSONAL STATEMENT

Raku cast its spell over me in the early 1970s, since then I have worked within its context almost continuously, with only a few excursions that did not include some component of my raku experience. Along the way I have tried a considerable variety of approaches and developed both forms and surfaces far beyond what might be

ABOVE: **'Arid Lands'**
(raku tea bowls,
iron nitrate/clear
glaze over).
PHOTO: G. HANCOCK

RIGHT: **'Drifting'**
(hand-made form,
matt black glaze).
PHOTO: M. KLUVANEK

considered typical of raku. Somehow, however, I seem to have come full circle and, after three decades, raku continues to surprise and fascinate. The reason is simple: raku is an adventure. It is a journey you embark on with great anticipation, drawn by the lure of the unexpected. It has its frustrations and disappointments, but always there remains the possibility that just around the corner there will be something extraordinary that will take your breath away. The best piece is always going to be the next!

Glaze Recipe: Superstition	
calcium borate frit	35
lithium carbonate	20
talc	30
nepheline-syenite	10
copper carbonate	3
cobalt carbonate	1–2

Blues through to deep reds with heavy reduction at 950–1000°C – wonderfully varied (figures are percentages by weight).

CAROL RATLIFF

Ratliff Pottery and Tile:
www.ratliffpotteryandtile.com

Carol, who lives in San Diego, in the USA, has kindly let me have this description of her use of the technique horsehair raku.

Using horsehair in a raku kiln differs from other raku techniques in that the piece is removed from the kiln at a low temperature, (+/–1200°F or +/–660°C), placed on the ground and horsehair is applied. You do not put it into a reduction chamber. The success depends on the type of clay used, the shape of the piece, the wind and, of course, the kiln gods. I use it on a burnished white clay piece that has a bit of grog in it in order to withstand the thermal shock the temperature changes will cause. I have used it on a red clay and tried it on glazed pieces, but I just prefer the blank canvas of a smooth, white, burnished pot. The horsehair makes its own pattern, depending on how much you use and the wind on that day. Try to fire on a calm day, as winds will just increase the chances that the piece may crack. Experiment and have fun.

'Desert Sky' (twice fired, iron chloride wash over clear glaze).
PHOTO: M. KLUVANEK

STEWART SCAMBLER

Studio: Palmyra, near Fremantle, W. Australia;
email: bohemian.ceramics@bigpond.com

Born in Scotland 1949 and emigrated to Western Australia in 1955. Educated at Fremantle Technical College and later at Edith Cowan University. Taught as sessional lecturer at technical colleges and universities around Perth. Stewart is presently President of the Ceramic Arts Association of Western Australia; he currently produces a range of majolica domestic ware, wood-fired stoneware and raku from a studio close to Fremantle.

Stewart and I have been friends for a number of years, having studied for our Batchelor of Arts degrees together at Edith Cowan University and exhibiting together in twelve or so exhibitions over ten years. Stewart has been a professional potter for over thirty years and has taught and given workshops throughout this period. He is renowned for his wood-fired pieces and his work may be found in several major collections, including the Art Gallery of Western Australia. I have included Stewart here because of his unusual method of post-firing reduction, which is accomplished without the use of a reduction container and by utilizing the ground for the sawdust or woodchips. Stewart places the reduction material on to the ground direct and then places the red hot work into this material, quickly covering it with wet newspapers. Any escaping smoke is quenched with yet more wet newspaper. This method is convenient when doing workshops since often there is little in the way of suitable containers available and it is safer for inexperienced people since there is no possibility of a flare-up when a drum is opened.

'Raku Smoked Vase'
(horsehair raku).

PERSONAL STATEMENT

For me there are similarities between the wood-fired stoneware and raku that I do. Both depend upon control and serendipity to produce the best work. In both techniques the process of making depends very much on the physical as well as the intellectual. My work is not overtly sculptural, rather it is based on vessel forms that can be pressed into service during the daily rituals of life.

I have very often used raku with students to introduce the idea that fire is an essential element of ceramic expression, and have them work directly with fire to loosen up and have them allow some random elements to influence their work, and to give them the feel and appreciation of the softness in raku work relative to stoneware. Indeed, it is the soft and quiet qualities of raku that I appreciate most. Mostly

I use a porcelain body bisqued to between 900 and 950°C. I fire in the top-hat gas-fired fibre kiln that I have had for the last twenty years. I use only a single white glaze, with occasionally a small strip of colour. My glaze fires to 950°C as I believe temperatures above this risk losing the soft qualities that I am seeking. I tend to reduce very lightly in the kiln and then transfer the work to a pile of hardwood sawdust and cover with layers of wet newspaper for post-firing reduction. Final cooling is achieved with a very fine spray of water.

Stewart Scambler's Favourite Glaze	
Percentage quantities:	
frit 4101	80
ball clay/kaolin	10
zirconium silicate	10

LISA SKEEN

Website: www.living-tree.net

I started working in clay in 1995, when I went back to college after a ten-year hiatus from formal education. In my English class, designed for adults and other 'non-traditional' students, one of our assignments was to learn something new and write about it. I signed up for a pottery class at the local recreation centre. The rest, as they say, is history. Most of my work has been functional stoneware, but I have also done a fair amount of work in alternative firing methods such as raku and pit firing.

My methods of creating horsehair raku pots have developed through trial and a lot of error. The pots are thrown on a potter's wheel, then trimmed when they are leather-hard and burnished using a Teflon rib. I use my Giffin Grip (an aid to hold work on a potter's wheel) for this process – the foam 'hands' are great for holding

OPPOSITE PAGE:
'Raku Bowl' (white crackle and copper).

THIS PAGE: **'Vase' (horsehair raku).**

pots in place while burnishing, without marring the surface, and it really speeds up the process considerably. After burnishing, when the pots are almost dry, I dip them in terra sigillata, which I then burnish with my fingertips. I do this several times to get a good coating. By the time they are ready for the kiln, they are quite shiny. My pieces are then bisque fired to cone 08. Many people say that one should not bisque that high for raku ware because the clay body will become too vitrified and will not take reduction smoke as well, but I have not had that problem.

What I use is a white porcelaineous stoneware clay body called Bee Mix, made by the Aardvark Clay Company. I started out using Laguna's B-Mix, but it became hard to get in my area, so I switched to the Aardvark brand. It fires very white and makes a really good ground for the horsehair treatment. Laguna's clay is available here in Australia but I don't know about the UK.

When first attempting horsehair raku, I fired the pieces up to about 1800°F (980°C) in a raku kiln outdoors. I quickly discovered what a mistake that was – because of the fine-grained clay body, the pots would not withstand the thermal shock of being pulled from the kiln and would literally pop into pieces while I was applying the hair. This was really frustrating to me. I have a low tolerance for failure and had about a 95 per cent loss with this method. I almost gave up because I did not want to use a coarse-grained raku clay body for horsehair work. Shortly thereafter, I was expressing my frustration in a conversation with my friend Charlie Riggs, of Riggs Pottery in Carthage, North Carolina. He has been making pots for over twenty-five years, and most of his work is either saggar-fired or raku. He said my mistake was firing outdoors where the wind and the open air could get to my pieces. He also said that I was firing way too hot for the process I was trying to use. I made a large batch of pots and hauled them down to Charlie's studio, where he and I fired them together, indoors, in his digitally controlled electric kiln. I

still use Charlie's method today and have almost zero losses as a result.

When firing horsehair raku, you want to take the same safety precautions you would for raku outdoors. This means wearing closed-toe shoes, long pants, long sleeves and goggles. A respirator is a great idea, because horsehair in a closed room is a really stinky operation. Do not forget to tie your hair back. Have all your materials laid out ahead of time and know where the pots are going to go when they are pulled from the kiln. The materials needed are raku gloves, raku tongs, a working partner, a propane torch and a safe place to put the pieces while they are still hot. It is also nice, but not absolutely necessary, to have a banding wheel with an insulation brick on top to place the pots on while working with them. You will also need some hair from the tail of a horse, pony or mule. Horsetail hair is thicker and coarser than human hair and contains an oil that makes the black carbon marks when placed on hot pots. My own hair is fairly long and I have used it on my pots, but the marks from human hair are very faint and thin. Make friends with the folks at the local petting zoo, or go to meet the new horse-owning neighbours. It is usually fairly easy, in my experience, to find someone with a horse. Using the long tail hairs has two advantages: the length goes further in wrapping around a pot and it keeps you from burning your fingers in the process.

After you have all your materials assembled and laid out, you and your partner need to decide who is going to do what task so that you will not run into each other in the process.

To get started, use kiln posts to raise the shelves high enough so that you don't have to reach deeply inside the kiln to pull your pieces out with the tongs. Place the pieces on the top shelf – it is no use having two layers, the kiln will be too hot to remove the shelves. I like to leave about an inch or so around each piece so that there is room to move the pot around when pulling them out without crashing into other

'Vases' (horsehair raku).

pots. Program the digital controller to ramp up to 1100°F (593°C). I set mine to do this in 2hr, and then hold for 2hr just to keep the temperature steady. When it is time to pull the pots out, it is time to close all the windows and doors and turn off the fans and air conditioning in the studio. You want as little air movement as possible to prevent breakage from thermal shock.

The insulation brick on top of the banding wheel is preheated with the propane torch. I wear one long raku gauntlet to raise the lid of the kiln while my partner Ginny pulls a pot from inside and places it on the banding wheel. While she is doing that, I close the lid, remove the glove and get busy applying horsehair. Some artists use clumps of horsehair. For me, single strands of hair work best and leave the most interesting marks, but it has to be done quickly. The pot is cooling rapidly while I'm working. My partner is meanwhile applying horsehair

on the side opposite to mine. When we think that we're done, we give the banding wheel a gentle spin just to be sure, then Ginny uses the raku tongs to move the pot to a table that we have covered with insulation bricks. This process is repeated until all the pots are done.

Since we have an ample supply of feathers at our place (we have several pet guinea fowl and chickens), I will often use feathers in addition to horsehair. The best feathers are the ones that are not stiff and that have kind of a loose structure in terms of the feather 'hairs'. One really interesting thing that we have found with guinea feathers is that their spots show up in the carbon marking.

After all the pots have cooled, I use a soft paintbrush to remove hair and feather crumbs and excess carbon. Each piece is then coated with clear paste floor wax (sometimes called bowling alley wax) and buffed to a soft shine before being sent to a gallery for sale.

135

SUBSTITUTE MATERIALS AND ALTERNATIVE NAMES, COLOURING OXIDES AND CONVERSIONS

SUBSTITUTE MATERIALS AND ALTERNATIVE NAMES

Many of the materials used in glazes go by a variety of names; the table *below* brings some of these together by country or area of use.

COLOURING OXIDES

To help you in creating glazes here are some colouring oxides and their range of colours:

Cobalt oxide, the strongest oxide, will give colours ranging from: 0.2 per cent, blue; 1–2

ALTERNATIVE NAMES BY COUNTRY		
Australia	**USA**	**Europe**
ball clay	OM4 ball clay; Tennessee ball clay	standard ball clay
bentonite	Macaloid suspension agent (similar to bentonite)	
China clay/kaolin	EPK	
fireclay	PBX fireclay	
potash feldspar	Buckingham feldspar; Kingman Custer	PBS potash feldspar Bell, G 200
red clay	Albany-type clay; Fremington-type clay	
soda feldspar	spruce pine # 4; Kona F-04	BPS soda feldspar
zirconium silicate	Zircopax; Opax; Superpax; any commercial opacifier	zircon

OPPOSITE: 'Shrine' (second view). PHOTO: VICTOR FRANCE

EFFECTS OF OXIDES IN VARYING PROPORTIONS

Minerals	Percentage	Possible Resulting Colours
chrome+vanadium	0.02–5	yellow–green
cobalt+chrome	0.02–2	blue–green
cobalt+rutile	0.05–15	blue–grey
cobalt+vanadium	0.05–10	yellow–mustard
copper+chrome	0.02–2	greens
copper+cobalt	0.02–2	blue–greens
copper+manganese	0.02–10	brown–black
copper+nickel	0.05–2	grey–green
copper+rutile	0.05–15	warm greens
copper+vanadium	0.05–10	yellow–green
iron+cobalt	0.01–10	grey–blue
iron+copper	0.05–0.2	green–black
iron+manganese	0.02–10	browns
iron+nickel	0.05–10	brown–grey
iron+rutile	0.01–10	yellow–browns
manganese+chrome	0.02–4	browns
manganese+cobalt	0.02–6	blue–purple
manganese+nickel	0.05–10	grey–browns
manganese+rutile	0.02–6	browns
manganese+vanadium	0.02–6	yellowish browns
nickel+chrome	0.02–2	browns
nickel+cobalt	0.05–3	grey–blue
nickel+rutile	0.02–2	browns
nickel+vanadium	0.05–10	yellow–brown

per cent, medium blue; 2–4 per cent, dark blue; and so forth till you get to almost black.

Copper oxide will give you green in oxidation and red in reduction.

Chromic oxide usually produces green, but if it is in a blend with tin oxide it is known to give pinks.

Ferric oxide has a broad range of colours, honey brown to yellow, through to brownish red and blacks.

Nickel oxide has a tendency to produce muted browns or greens, but nickel and chrome will give you softer greens.

Manganese dioxide is quite weak in contrast to the other oxides; colours range from medium to dark brown; you can achieve a plum or purple if the oxide added to a high alkaline glaze.

Rutile is titanium oxide ore; useful as a modifier in glazes containing iron, copper, cobalt or chrome.

Vanadium pentoxide used mainly in stains since the colours produced are more stable.

The table on p.138 shows the effects of using these oxides in varying proportions. Make a line blend and test to get precise results and keep an accurate record of each test for future use. This is only some of the oxides it is possible to use and their colours; experiment with different combined oxides, but remember that firing in an oxidation or a reduction can often change the result. Use the first ingredient in the table, then add, by increments, the second.

CONVERSIONS

FAHRENHEIT TO CELSIUS CONVERSION					
°F	°C	°F	°C	°F	°C
1	−17	100	38	1900	1037
2	−17	200	93	2000	1091
3	−16	300	149	2100	1148
4	−16	400	204	2200	1203
5	−15	500	260	2300	1259
6	−14	600	315	2400	1314
7	−14	700	371	2500	1370
8	−13	800	426	2600	1425
9	−13	900	482	2700	1481
10	−12	1000	537	2800	1536
20	−7	1100	593	2900	1592
30	−1	1200	648	3000	1647
40	4	1300	704	3100	1703
50	10	1400	759	3200	1758
60	16	1500	815	3300	1814
70	21	1600	870	3400	1869
80	27	1700	926	3500	1925
90	32	1800	981	3600	1980

WEIGHTS AND MEASURES CONVERSIONS FROM METRIC TO IMPERIAL

1g = 0.035oz	1ltr = 33.81fl oz
1g = 0.0022lb	1ltr = 1.76 pints
1kg = 35.27oz	1ltr = 0.88 quarts
1kg = 2.20lb	1mm = 0.039in
1ml = 0.034fl oz	1cm = 0.394in
	1m = 39.37in

WEIGHTS AND MEASURES CONVERSIONS FROM IMPERIAL TO METRIC

1oz = 28.35g	1ft = 30.48cm
1lb = 453.6g	1yd = 91.44cm
1st = 6.3503kg	1 mile = 1.61km
1 hundredweight	1fl oz = 28.413ml
(cwt) = 50.802kg	1pt = 568.3ml
1in = 2.54cm	1gal = 4.546ltr

BIBLIOGRAPHY

The following sources, some of the wide range of available materials, are the ones I found to be the most helpful in writing this book.

BOOKS

Andrews, Tim, *A Review of Contemporary Raku* (A. & C. Black, London, 1997)

Birks, Tony, *The Complete Potter's Companion* (Conran Octopus, London, 1997)

Branfman, Steven, *Raku: A Practical Approach* (A. & C. Black, London, 1991)

Branfman, Steven, *The Potter's Professional Handbook* (American Ceramic Society, 1996)

Byers, Ian, *Raku: The Complete Potter* (Kangaroo Press, Kenthurst, Australia, 1990)

Connell, Jo, *The Potter's Guide to Ceramic Surfaces* (New Burlington Books, London, 2002)

Ferguson, Gary, *Raku Glazes: The Ultimate Collection; Over 360 Recipes and More* (self-published, 2003)

Ferguson, Gary, *Raku Secrets: The Complete Guide of Amazing Raku Results* (self-published, 2004)

Jones, David, *Raku: Investigations into Fire* (The Crowood Press, Ramsbury, 1999)

Nigrosh, Leon, *Clayworks: Form and Idea in Ceramic Design* (Davis Publishers, Worcester, MA, 1995)

Peterson, Susan, *The Craft and Art of Clay* (Laurance King Publishers, London, 1992)

Sentence, Bryan, *Ceramics: A World Guide to Traditional Techniques* (Thames & Hudson, London, 2004)

Watkins, James C. & Paul A. Wandless, *Alternative Kilns and Firing techniques* (Lark Books, New York, 2004)

PERIODICAL LITERATURE

Ceramic Art & Perception (Sydney, Australia)

Ceramic Technical (Sydney, Australia)

Craft Arts International (Sydney, Australia)

Pottery in Australia (The Potters Society, Crows Nest, Australia)

GLOSSARY

Albany Slip slip made from Albany clay; produces yellows, blacks and browns over a wide temperature range.

Ball clay sedimentary clay used in white earthenware, china and porcelain bodies, engobes and many glaze recipes.

Base glaze basic components that are used in a particular glaze; oxides are added to this to provide the colours.

Bisque or biscuit unglazed but fired ware, usually fired at a low temperature before a glaze firing.

Blowtorch usually a hand-held appliance powered from an LPG gas bottle.

Body combination of natural and non-plastic clays, especially formulated to have certain workability and firing characteristics.

Bone ash mineral calcium phosphate or ash from bones; found in Europe and the Orient and used in clay bodies or as a glaze flux.

Borax main source of boric oxide for use in glazes; usually used as a frit.

Carbonate for instance, copper carbonate or cobalt carbonate; used as a colourant in glazes; sometimes referred to as carb.; a compound of minerals that is not as concentrated as the oxide.

China clay primary or secondary kaolin; refractory, not very plastic.

Coiling traditional method of using clay in long rolls to hand-build a hollow form.

Combustibles inflammable materials such as wood or paper.

Cuprous, cupric common names for the copper (I) and (II) valency states.

Damper adjustable shutter to control the draft or flue in a kiln.

Engobe slip coloured with oxides or glaze stains, can be applied to either wet or leather-hard ware as decoration; may be used under a glaze.

Feldspar mineral found in granite and used as a flux in clay bodies and glazes.

Ferric oxide red iron oxide, Fe_2O_3.

Ferrous, ferric common names for the iron (II) and (III) valency states.

Fireclay refractory clay often used in kilns and as fire bricks, high in alumina.

Flux an oxide used as a fusion in a glaze, most often an alkaline oxide, but exceptions are boric and bismuth oxides; a mixture that has a low melting point.

Frit part of a glaze recipe that has been melted and reground; often this is to render the minerals less volatile; lead, antimony, barium and zinc are some of the materials used as frits; may consist of two or more materials together to give a more stable and less toxic product.

Fuming use of a chemical, most often a chloride, to produce special effects by introducing them into the kiln, either placing them near the work or in a spoon attached to a long rod which is inserted into the firing chamber.

Grog ground, fired body added to clays to provide a texture and to help in forming a piece of work; grog is also considered an opener which helps to control the uneven drying of a clay; most often used in a raku body to assist with the thermal shock and prevent cracking.

Leather-hard clay that is stiff and can support itself, but which is still soft enough to be altered.

Lustre technique developed in Persia and Valencia during the Middle Ages; produces iridescent, metallic colours through the use of metallic salts under reduction.

Matt non-reflective surface on a glaze.

Maturing temperature that the clay or glaze needs to reach to obtain the results desired.

Mica any of a group of silicate minerals with a layered structure.

Opacifiers minerals included in a glaze to aid in opacity; the opacifier does not readily dissolve in the molten glaze; tin oxide is the most popular.

Oxidation, oxidizing fire opposite of reduction firing; the combustion of fuel is complete.

Patina surface effect developed over time or has been aided by chemicals; in ceramics this is often an unusual effect obtained during firing.

Petalite silicate of lithium and aluminium used in glazes; pure petalite, like spodumene, has a low expansion rate.

Porcelain white, translucent, high-fired stoneware clay usually fired to 1300°C.

Pyrometer instrument to measure kiln temperature; most often used in conjunction with a thermocouple.

Quartz crystalline silica (SiO_2); occurs as milky quartz and crystal quartz; used as a source of silica for glazes.

Rainbow effect thin layers of silver, bismuth, copper or tin on the surface of glazes which may present lustres and rainbow or mother-of-pearl colours.

Reduction opposite of oxidizing firing; fuel combustion is incomplete.

Resist decorative technique achieved by using wax or paper placed over the piece to prevent a covering of glaze or slip in a particular area; the wax or paper is either removed or left to burn off in the kiln.

Shards pottery fragments.

Sieve frame holding a mesh across it; used to separate coarse materials in glaze or slip materials, exist in many sizes.

Sgraffito decorative technique using lines scratched into an area of the work; usually a lighter colour is scratched to reveal a darker colour underneath.

Slip mixture of clay and water with the addition of other materials to assist the slip to fit the body; slips may be coloured with oxides and are also used as a slip-glaze, which contains approximately 50 per cent clay.

Slip-cast pottery-making technique using moulds to create the pieces; the clay is poured into the moulds while it is in the form of a slip.

Spodumene silicate of lithium and aluminium, used in bodies and glazes.

Suspender material added to a glaze to keep materials in suspension; most commonly used is bentonite.

Terra-sigillata very fine ground clay suspended in water; after coating and burnishing a piece with this it will result in a sheen following a low-temperature firing.

Viscosity measure of fluidity of a glaze; a low viscosity produces a flow and usually results in a gloss finish; a high viscosity glaze is 'stiff' and usually produces a matt finish.

Vitrification stage during firing at which a clay body is no longer able to collapse onto itself; a fully-fired clay.